Managing Fore
Exchange Risk

Managing Foreign Exchange Risk

How to identify and manage foreign currency exposure

DOMINIC BENNETT

FT PITMAN PUBLISHING

London · Hong Kong · Johannesburg
Melbourne · Singapore · Washington DC

PITMAN PUBLISHING
128 Long Acre, London WC2E 9AN
Tel: +44 (0)171 447 2000
Fax: +44 (0)171 240 5771

A Division of Pearson Professional Limited

First published in Great Britain 1997

ISBN 0 273 61976 4

British Library Cataloguing in Publication Data
A CIP catalogue record for this book can be obtained from the British Library.

10 9 8 7 6 5 4 3 2 1

Typeset by Northern Phototypesetting Co. Ltd., Bolton
Printed and bound in Great Britain by Bell and Bain Ltd, Glasgow

The Publishers' policy is to use paper manufactured from sustainable forests.

About the Author

Dominic Bennett graduated from London University with a degree in history in 1974. He then joined Ford Motor Company as a financial analyst and held a number of positions in the Ford of Europe finance function. In 1977 he entered the Ford of Europe treasury department where he was primarily responsible for foreign exchange management, the investment of surplus cash, cashflow forecasting and management reporting. In this role, Dominic managed Ford's intercompany currency netting processes and arranged hedging of the net exposures. In 1982 he joined the group treasury of Reed International and was responsible for developing and managing its investment, borrowing and foreign exchange dealing activities during a period of rapid change in the group that involved a number of major acquisitions and divestments.

Dominic was appointed Treasurer – Financial Services Unit at Griffin (London) Limited in 1986. The company, part of a privately owned Australian group, was involved in commodity trading in Australia and the Pacific Rim, and Dominic was responsible for dealing in exotic currencies and managing the uncertain timing of payments which became due when cargo ships arrived in port after voyages of several weeks' duration.

In 1988, he joined the corporate treasury team within KPMG's management consultancy practice. Since that time he has advised a wide range of clients on all aspects of treasury management and in particular on foreign exchange policies, strategies, dealing processes and controls. Dominic is a member of the Association of Corporate Treasurers and lectures on treasury management matters for a number of organizations. He has written articles that have been published in magazines in both the UK and the USA. He is also a co-author (with KPMG colleagues) of *Organising and Controlling your Treasury* (Pitman Publishing, 1994).

Contents

Introduction

....

This is not a book for speculators. It is intended primarily to help those who, as a result of their commercial activities, have to manage foreign currency risk; although I hope students will also find it useful. The emphasis of the book therefore is not on making profit from foreign exchange dealing but on practical issues involved in managing currency risk.

Having been involved with corporate treasury management for nearly 20 years in a variety of organizations and roles, I am conscious that it is a discipline that is subject to constant change through, for example, the development of new hedging instruments, changes to the tax and accounting treatment of hedging transactions, and government policies. In the time that I have been actively involved in currency management I have seen the introduction of currency options and associated derivatives, the abolition of exchange controls over Sterling, Sterling's membership of the Exchange Rate Mechanism of the European Monetary System and suspension from it, and changes to the accounting treatment of hedging transactions. In addition, we have seen, and continue to see, fundamental changes in business and treasury activity around the world as new markets open up and international banking systems develop to service them. At the time of writing, the debate about the Single European Currency continues and, if anything, is likely to intensify as the dates set at Maastricht for the stages in the process draw nearer. My experience has chiefly been gained in the UK; other countries will have had similar issues and events which have affected both the ability to manage currency exposure and the implications to be considered in doing so.

In view of this constant change and my desire to make this book as widely applicable as possible, I have deliberately not covered the accounting, taxation and regulatory aspects of currency management as these are matters which vary from country to country and can change rapidly. Instead, I have focused on what I believe are the unchanging and widely applicable fundamentals of exposure identification and management. In particular, I wanted to make this book useful for smaller companies that do not have the resources to run a sophisticated treasury function but still need to manage currency exposure efficiently.

I know from my experience of talking to, and advising, such companies that there is a desire to understand not just about hedging instruments but about the wider and more fundamental issues relating to currency exposure management. I have tried to discuss these issues in layman's terms, avoiding mathematical formulae and explaining the jargon where it is necessary to use it.

In order to help those who are coming to foreign exchange management for the first time, I have assumed that the reader has no previous understanding or expertise in the subject. I beg the forbearance of those with more experience who may find that the earlier chapters confirm what they already know rather than shed new light, but I believe that it is essential to have a clear understanding of the nature of currency exposure and how to identify it *before* reaching for a hedging instrument. I hope, however, that all readers, whatever their level of knowledge will find something of value in this book.

In writing this book I am greatly indebted to Valerie Hawkes, a treasury practitioner and consultant of wide experience, who read through the manuscript and made many helpful comments and suggestions. Any errors or omissions that remain in this book (and I hope there are none) are, however, mine alone.

Dominic Bennett,
November 1996

Part One

1 The background –
history and economics

2 Quantifying exposure and risk

3 Policies and organization

Governmental and international attempts to stabilize exchange rates have a long history

The background – history and economics

- The Gold Standard
- The Bretton Woods system
- The rise of the Dollar
- The 1950s and 1960s
- The collapse of the Bretton Woods system
- The Smithsonian Agreement
- The European Monetary System
- Why do exchange rates move?

In essence, currency exposure management is about managing the *effects* of movements in exchange rates. Clearly, a basic understanding of the factors that produce such movements would provide a useful background for the management of currency risk. In this chapter we look briefly at the history of governmental attempts to stabilize foreign exchange rates over the past 100 years or so, identify the difficulties encountered in attempting to do so, and highlight the factors responsible for movements in exchange rates.

The Gold Standard

The history of governmental and international attempts to stabilize exchange rates is a long one. Early monetary systems used both gold and silver prices as reference values but, eventually, in 1880 the Gold Standard, using gold alone, was established. The Gold Standard was a system of fixed exchange rates whose parities were set in relation to gold. It was composed of two elements: the Gold Specie Standard and the Gold Bullion Standard.

The Gold Specie Standard gave gold two roles; as a recognized means of payment for the settlement of international liabilities and, in the form of gold coins, as the one accepted domestic medium of exchange. In order for gold to fulfil these roles it was necessary for four conditions to be satisfied:

- Central banks had to guarantee to buy or sell gold in unrestricted amounts at a fixed price.
- Anyone should be permitted to melt gold down and use it for a different purpose.
- A holder of gold must be able to have coin struck from bullion in any amount, and
- There must be no restrictions on the import and export of gold.

These conditions were designed to ensure that the face value and bullion value of the coinage were always the same. Under the Gold Specie Standard, liquidity was determined by the rate of gold production and the use of gold for industrial purposes.

Under the Gold Bullion Standard, gold acted as a reserve asset and paper money could be exchanged for gold at the bank of issue. Since it was likely that only a small proportion of paper money would be exchanged for gold, the bank could issue paper money with a value of several times the amount of gold held. The lower that the rate of coverage was fixed, the greater was the amount of paper money that could be issued.

The operation of the Gold Standard had a direct impact on international payments. A country with a balance of payments deficit had to surrender gold; this led to a reduction in the volume of money and resulted in deflation. At the same time, the inflow of gold into the country in surplus caused inflation. The resulting difference in price levels enabled the deficit country to increase its exports and reduce its imports and thereby to improve its balance of payments. This was usually accompanied by the deficit country raising, and the surplus country lowering, its discount rate. The movements of capital which resulted tended to bring the payments between the two countries into balance.

Under the Gold Standard, exchange rates were only permitted to fluctuate between the limits known as the upper and lower gold points. Variances from the official gold rate arose because the physical transfer of gold involved freight and insurance costs. If the exchange rate for any currency rose above its parity value so that it became cheaper to ship gold than to purchase the currency, a debtor would exchange his money and make payment in gold. If, on the other hand, a currency weakened, a creditor could demand to be paid in gold.

The First World War seriously affected the operation of the Gold Standard because the restrictions that it imposed on the creation of money conflicted with the unprecedented financing requirements of the combatants. As a result, many countries found ways to circumvent the rules imposed by the Gold Standard. Attempts by some countries to reintro-

> *The operation of the Gold Standard had a direct impact on international payments.*

duce gold currency failed because a number of the major countries would have been under- or over-valued. By 1933, only France, Belgium, Holland, Italy and Switzerland still remained on the Gold Standard, and in 1936 the devaluation of the French and Swiss Francs heralded the end of the system.

After the First World War, differing inflation rates made it increasingly difficult to adhere to the exchange parities of the Gold Standard and a number of countries were forced to devalue. The effect of this, however, was to cause those countries which had not devalued (and had in effect been revalued) to devalue in their turn in an attempt to restore the previous parity. All the major currencies participated in the devaluation spiral. As the world economic crisis developed in the 1930s, governments began to introduce exchange controls to ensure that there were sufficient reserves available to pay for essential commodities. To achieve this, they had to control the import and export of foreign exchange: to this end, they typically introduced controls over the export of capital and the requirement for international traders to surrender to the state the foreign currency proceeds of their business.

The Bretton Woods system

The mechanism for ensuring exchange rate stability was inspired by establishment of the Gold Standard.

In 1943, Great Britain and the USA, fearing a return to the problems of the inter-war years, began the process that was to lead to the establishment of the Gold Exchange Standard and the International Monetary Fund (IMF).

At the Bretton Woods conference in 1944 the objectives of the new monetary system were set out. These can be summarized as follows:

- to establish an international monetary system with stable exchange rates
- to eliminate exchange controls, and
- to achieve convertibility for all currencies.

The basic mechanism for ensuring stability of exchange rates (within a fixed range of fluctuation above a particular parity) owed its inspiration to the Gold Standard. Each member of the IMF set a parity for its currency relative to gold or the Dollar and agreed to limit fluctuations to within 1 per cent of the parity by central bank market intervention. It was also agreed that any change in parities had to be approved by the IMF; however, this approval could not be refused if the change were less than 10 per cent.

The rise of the Dollar

The Bretton Woods system established the Dollar as the major world currency in three respects:

- The Dollar was confirmed as the major reserve currency. In 1944 the United States gave an undertaking to the IMF that it would buy and sell gold with other monetary authorities at a price of $35 per ounce. This guaranteed that the Dollar could be converted into gold and, as a result, most countries began to hold their reserves in both gold and Dollars.

- Because of its convertibility into gold, the Dollar also served as a parity reference and most central banks bought and sold it when intervening to keep their own currencies within the prescribed limits.
- The Dollar also became the main currency for the settlement of international transactions and the pricing of major commodities.

The 1950s and 1960s

The Bretton Woods system was effective for about 25 years, although there were occasional crises and problems. Throughout most of the 1950s the international currency scene was reasonably calm and progress was made towards the objectives of the Bretton Woods system. In December 1958, the European Monetary Agreement came into force and convertibility (to a greater or lesser extent) was introduced for western European currencies. At the end of 1958, however, the USA's huge balance of payments deficits started a run on gold, and the price rose above $35 per ounce for the first time since 1951. The central banks had to step in to resolve the crisis by establishing a gold pool and stabilizing the price by market intervention.

The 1960s, however, saw gathering difficulties, caused largely by the difference in growth rates between individual countries. In March 1961, as a result of large balance of payments surpluses in Germany and Holland, the Deutsche Mark and Dutch Guilder were revalued. Sterling, on the other hand, was coming under pressure and after prolonged support was finally devalued in 1967 from $2.80 to $2.40. Throughout the remainder of the 1960s there were further stresses. The May 1968 riots in Paris caused such a loss of confidence in the French Franc that the Banque de France used up so much of its currency reserves in supporting it that it eventually had

The European Monetary Agreement and western European currency convertibility came into force in December 1958.

to devalue it by 11 per cent in August 1969. The Deutsche Mark, on the other hand, was suffering pressure in the other direction. A huge inflow of capital into the Mark forced the Bundesbank in September 1969 to

7

cease its intervention in the market and let the currency float for a short time. A month later, the Mark was revalued by 9.3 per cent.

The collapse of the Bretton Woods system

The early 1970s saw a loss of confidence in the Dollar, due chiefly to the massive US balance of payments deficits. During the 1960s these deficits had been responsible for reducing the US's gold reserves from $18 billion in 1960 to $11 billion in 1970. By 1970, also, foreign official short-term claims on the USA were more than double its gold reserve. As a result, the Dollar's convertibility into gold was increasingly brought into question.

With confidence in the Dollar under attack, a decline in US interest rates from 1970 set off a Dollar crisis at the beginning of 1971. A massive capital outflow from the US took place, seeking higher interest rates in Europe. This forced the major European central banks initially to intervene in the markets and then either to revalue (in the case of Switzerland and Austria) or, like Germany and Holland, to float. The Dollar crisis continued, however, and by August 1971 the US finally abandoned Dollar–gold convertibility. In response, most other countries joined Germany and Holland and let their currencies float.

The Smithsonian Agreement

One final, ill-fated, attempt was made to rescue the principles of Bretton Woods. The Smithsonian Agreement of December 1971 attempted to establish a realignment of the major currencies and a return to fixed parities. The USA agreed to raise the official gold price to $38 per ounce (in effect a devaluation of the Dollar) and, in response, Japan and the European countries agreed to revalue by up to 7.66 per cent. The intervention points were widened to 2.25 per cent either side of parity, enabling the non-Dollar currencies to fluctuate against each other by up to 4.5 per cent.

The key weakness of the Smithsonian Agreement was, however, that the Dollar's convertibility into gold had not been reinstated. The realignment of exchange rates helped to stabilize the situation for a time, but speculative capital movements soon reappeared. By June 1972 Sterling was under pressure and the British Government was forced to let it float. In January 1973 it was the turn of the Lira and the Italian government responded by splitting it into a commercial and financial Lira in order to exercise greater control. Switzerland, in the same month, let the Franc float for a while under

The 'snake' was established to set and maintain agreed parities.

the pressure of massive capital inflows. In February 1973 the US devalued again and raised the gold price to $42.22. This failed to stop the outflow of capital, however, and in March 1973 Japan and the European hard-currency countries announced that they would no longer intervene in the market. This action marked the demise of the Bretton Woods system.

The European Monetary System

After the collapse of the Smithsonian Agreement it was felt in Europe that exchange rate stability was still a desirable objective and that there was yet a role for some form of formal international mechanism to achieve this. As a result, the 'snake' was established in order to set and maintain agreed parities. At its inception it comprised most of the EEC currencies (but not Sterling) and the Swedish Krona.

By 1979 the snake was left with only a small core of its original members. On an initiative of the President of France and the German Chancellor, however, it was about to undergo a transformation into the European Monetary System, the two key features of which were:

- the limited pooling of foreign exchange reserves which all EEC members participated in, and
- the establishment of an exchange rate mechanism (ERM).

The ERM established the European Currency Unit (replacing in the process the European Unit of Account). The ECU was defined as a basket of EEC Member currencies, the proportions of which were weighted according to the Members' gross domestic products. Each currency was given a parity against the ECU and had to remain within specified percentage bands of the parity. In doing this, parities *between* Member currencies were determined and it was laid down that parities between Member currencies were not allowed to diverge by more than the same percentage. In fact, it was envisaged that if the divergence reached 75 per cent of the permitted divergence the Member central banks involved would intervene to bring the currencies back to the parity. To assist this, facilities were to be granted to give the relevant central banks access to the required currency reserves.

The ERM was established with two bands: 2.25 per cent for the majority of countries and 6 per cent for those requiring more room for manoeuvre. The broad, 6 per cent, band was intended to be temporary but, in practice, it became a longstanding feature of the ERM. To some extent, it is true to say that those countries in the broad band tended to regard themselves as second-class members of the ERM and were generally keen to advance to narrow band status.

It is possible to chart a number of stages in the development of the ERM:

● In the first stage there were frequent devaluations as members sought to maintain stability.

● In the second stage, central banks (perhaps in recognition of the constraints of the system) did not devalue enough to compensate fully for movements in relative price levels, with the aim of using foreign competitive pressure to push down domestic inflation.

● A third stage, in which devaluation was considered a national disgrace and was used only as a last resort.

   Germany was seen as the role model and her example could be copied by using the Deutsche Mark as a parallel currency. The result of this was that a number of countries within the ERM tied themselves tightly to the Mark, while others outside the ERM tied themselves informally to it.

● A fourth stage, encompassing Sterling's entry to, and suspension from, the ERM.

The ERM is now firmly established and attention has now moved on in Europe to focus on proposals for economic and monetary union (EMU). The introduction of a single European currency is the means by which EMU is intended to be achieved. Clearly, a single currency has political, economic and social implications that are far more significant than those of a system of linked, but adjustable, national currencies.

This book is not the proper place to debate the advantages and disadvantages of a single currency or whether it will ever become a reality. It is appropriate, however, to point out that in planning for EMU the proponents of a single currency have recognized that the concept can only succeed if the economic performance of each of the participating states meets, and continues to meet, specified criteria. In other words, it is recognized that currency movements over time are primarily caused by differences in economic performance (as discussed later in this chapter) and unless these differences are eliminated by the convergence of the economies of the participating countries the single currency will not be viable.

The Treaty on European Union, which was signed at Maastricht in February 1992, mapped the path to EMU in three phases. Phase A, which includes the formal decision to move to EMU by the qualified states, can only commence if individual states meet the five specified economic criteria. These criteria relate to inflation, long-term interest rates, exchange rates, government deficits (not to exceed 60 per cent of GDP) and debt (not more than 3 per cent of GDP).

Phase B is intended to begin on 1 January 1999. Its key features are the locking of the exchange rates of the participating currencies and the beginning of single currency activities, principally through the European Central Bank. It is expected that Phase B will last for a number of years to give time for changes to the banking system to be implemented and for notes and coins to be produced and distributed.

> *Differences in economic performance between participating countries need to be eliminated if the single currency is to be viable.*

Phase C would complete the process by the conversion of national currencies into the single currency.

Why do exchange rates move?

It will be seen from the above brief outline of the history of attempts to manage exchange rate stability that certain themes recur: the effects over time of the balance of payments, capital flows, inflation and growth rates. These are the economic fundamentals that sooner or later assert themselves and, where an attempt formally or informally has been made to fix rates at an historical parity, administer a shock to the system to bring them into line again with what the market considers to be economic reality. An understanding of how long-term economic fundamentals interrelate with short-term political, or other, factors is essential to understanding both why exchange rates move and the rationale behind the forecasts made by economists.

The movements over time in the exchange rate of a *freely floating* currency should be viewed as having two key constituents. One, economic performance, can be considered to be the foundation of the trend of the currency in relation to other currencies. The other, short-term political and other transient factors, largely accounts for the volatility around the long-term trend line.

The short-term political factors that can affect a currency are well known to most participants in, and observers of, the financial markets: elections, coups, assassination attempts, deaths of leading politicians, coalitions falling apart, a general lack of confidence in a government, even adverse opinion polls. These can deliver shocks to a currency; but these shocks are generally short lived and followed by a correction in rates. These short-term shocks are, by their nature, difficult both to predict and to quantify in terms of their likely impact on exchange rates. Economic factors, reflecting longer-term trends, are (arguably) easier to forecast and to quantify in terms of the value in the longer term of a currency *vis à vis* other currencies.

The theory of purchasing power parity

The purchasing power parity theory holds that freely floating exchange rates are affected predominantly by differences in inflation rates. Thus, a currency with a high inflation rate can be expected to depreciate against one with a lower inflation rate, to maintain the purchasing power of the two currencies so that the price of goods in the two countries concerned is the same.

A simple example of the working of the theory can be given in the case of two countries (A and B) who, at the beginning of Year 1, have a A1.00 = B1.00 exchange rate. At the end of Year 1, inflation in Country A has been 10 per cent and inflation in Country B has been 5 per cent. Because the price of goods in Country A has increased at a faster rate than in Country B, Country B will require an appreciation in its currency versus that of Country A to maintain its purchasing power parity.

Thus, Country B's currency would have to appreciate against that of Country A (and A's depreciate against that of B) by 110 – 105 to maintain B's purchasing power. The new rate of exchange so derived is A1.0476 = B1.00. At this rate the cost of goods priced at A1.1000 is B1.0500. Purchasing power parity has been maintained because the currency of A depreciated by the differential in the inflation rates between A and B.

The theory of purchasing power parity can be shown to have some basis in fact. There are, however, a number of considerations that must be borne in mind when using purchasing power parity as the basis for explaining exchange rate movements. These are:

● Price indices are not prepared on the same basis in each country and most countries use more than one index. Care should be taken, therefore, that the indices used are understood before conclusions are drawn about their effect on exchange rate movements.

● The only prices that should affect exchange rates are those that relate to goods and services that can be traded internationally. A rise in purely domestic costs, such as housing rent or mortgage costs, may be reflected in a price index but should not have a direct impact on exchange rates (it may, however, have an indirect short-term effect if it contributes to a perception of an unfavourable political environment).

> *Purchasing power parity is useful for explaining long-term currency trends.*

● Factors other than price can be equally, or more, important to a country's international competitiveness. Quality, speed of delivery, and after-sales service can all help an individual exporter (or exporting country) to maintain or even increase its market share regardless of price considerations. Where a price increase does not result in a commensurate fall in sales, the net effect will be an increase in demand for the exporter's currency as importers require more of it.

Purchasing power parity therefore, while being useful for explaining long-term currency trends, has its shortcomings as a tool for shorter-term exposure management. Some economists consider a country's current account balance to be a better guide to likely exchange rate trends in the shorter time horizon (up to 12 months) that most market operators are involved in. The current account balance, comprising goods, services, investment income and transfers, is held to be a reasonably fair indicator of a country's international competitiveness. A current account surplus (that is, a net inflow of overseas earnings), creating a net demand for the country's currency, will have the effect of strengthening it. A deficit will have the opposite effect. The current account balance, as one would expect with a broader and more complex measure than purchasing power parity, is dependent upon, and affected by, a wider range of factors. These factors include:

The current account balance

● Inflation. If inflation is higher in a particular country than elsewhere, its international competitiveness will be weakened. As noted above, all other things being equal, this will eventually lead to a fall in exports and a rise in imports.

- A comparatively high economic growth rate. This typically results in an increase in imports (both of raw materials and finished goods) to satisfy domestic needs. At the same time, the trend of exports, which are affected by weaker economic performance in other countries, grows more slowly or remains flat.

In both of the above circumstances the trade balance will eventually worsen, and demand for a country's currency for trading purposes will decrease. However, trading flows arising from the international exchange of goods and services (including interest) are only part of the story: movements in the capital account must also be put into the equation.

The effect of capital flows

In the past, flows of capital from one country to another were insignificant when compared with the trade, services and interest flows that make up the current account balance. The two main reasons for this were the comparatively low level of liquid savings worldwide and the restrictions, through exchange controls, on the freedom of movement of these assets. As we discussed above, since the 1970s there has been a general relaxation of exchange controls (particularly in those countries in which high levels of liquid savings are concentrated) while, at the same time, the level of savings has risen dramatically. As a result, capital flows can now have as much, or even more, effect on exchange rates than current account flows.

As a general rule, investors of capital will seek the highest return. This is one reason why a government will use interest rate rises to protect or strengthen its currency; capital is attracted, thereby increasing demand for the currency. Investors recognize, however, that in a floating exchange rate system they are exposed to exchange losses if the currency weakens. They therefore take into account their expectations for any exchange rate movements in calculating the projected net return on their investments and may decide that, although the nominal interest rate for a currency is attractive, the risk of depreciation in the currency outweighs the interest rate advantage. Capital flows can also be the cause of major and sudden exchange rate movements as, in contrast to the flows that make up the trade balance, they can be reversed and may change direction at short notice.

> *Investors of capital will seek the highest return.*

While most economists agree that economic factors determine long-term trends in exchange rates, they recognize the influence, as we noted earlier, of political and psychological factors in the shorter term. The chief effects of these short-term factors are to influence capital flows from weak or low yielding currencies into those that are considered safer or which offer the prospect of a better overall return. Other considerations that can affect currencies in the short term include regulatory restrictions on banks' open positions and minimum reserve requirements that must be met on specified reporting dates. Both of these can create a sudden (but technical) demand for a currency that results in a temporary strengthening of its rate.

Short-term factors

Another cause of short-term movements in rates is the influence of technical analysts on the market. The short-term forecasts produced by analysts using charts, momentum models and moving averages are acted upon by dealers and can, for short periods, be the dominant influence on exchange rates. The role of technical analysis in forecasting exchange rates is discussed in more detail in Chapter 2.

The task, and challenge, for those responsible for managing currency exposure is to understand all the factors responsible for exchange movements, both in the short and the longer term, to interpret the signals given by the market and to respond by taking action that is appropriate to the significance of the risk that is faced and is consistent with the risk appetite of the organization. This requires an appreciation of the nature and size of the organization's currency exposures, and the potential for adverse exchange rate movements, and an assessment of their potential effect. These fundamental elements in the currency exposure management process are discussed in detail in the next chapter.

Summary

In this chapter I have discussed how governments have attempted in the past to control exchange rate movements and how differences in economic performance between countries have led to exchange rate fluctuations.

An understanding of the effects of economic fundamentals on exchange rates can form the basis of a methodology for forecasting future exchange rates. The use of forecasted economic data, on the one hand, and price history on the other, for forecasting future exchange rates is discussed in the next chapter.

Can forecast currency flows be considered as exposures?

Quantifying exposure and risk

- What is a currency exposure?
- Translation exposure
- Transaction exposure
- Economic exposure
- Forecasting currency exposure
- Forecasting exchange rates
- Quantifying currency risk

In this chapter we will consider the elements that comprise foreign exchange risk, and how they can be identified and quantified. There are two facets to this: the nature and quantum of the *exposure* and the potential for exchange rate movements. These two elements combine to produce the currency *risk* faced by an organization. The questions that those who are responsible for managing currency risk should ask themselves are:

- What is currency exposure and what types of exposure do I have?
- What are the amounts, timing and currencies of my exposures?
- What effect could the exposure have on my business if I do not manage it?

Before answering these questions it is worth pausing for a moment to consider two other questions:

- **What is a currency?** In most respects the answer to this is the same as the definition of money: a medium of exchange, a store of value and a unit of account. Where currency differs from money, in most people's minds, is that it is foreign money and that, as such, its role as a store of value will be affected by movements in the exchange rate between it and the domestic currency; and

- **What is an exchange rate?** An exchange rate is the price of one currency in terms of another. Currencies are commodities and (in the absence of government-imposed restrictions) are traded in a market in much the same way as other commodities. The rate of exchange for a currency will, at any time, be determined by a range of factors – economic, political and commercial – all of which will affect the demand for the currency and thus its exchange rate.

What is a currency exposure?

Let us now return to our original question: what is currency exposure? In simple terms, we can define it as a current position or a committed or forecast future asset or liability denominated in a foreign currency which either for trading (profit and loss account) or balance sheet purposes will have to be converted or translated into another currency at a rate which is yet to be determined.

Exposures will therefore include:

- foreign currency denominated items in the balance sheet
- actual, physical purchases and sales of goods and services which have yet to be invoiced
- contracted purchases and sales, such as long-term contracts to purchase capital equipment, and
- uncontracted foreign currency denominated receipts and payments which will materialize if forecasted trading activity is realized.

The wording of the above definition includes a point which requires further discussion.

There is a continuing debate among corporate treasurers as to whether forecast, as opposed to actual or committed, exposures can truly be considered to be exposures. Strictly speaking, of course, they are not exposures as they do not represent an actual position or contractual commitment. However, to ignore them would be to deny oneself the ability to identify and manage, in advance, likely future risks. Such exposures could then only be managed as they crystallized, by which time it would be too late to protect against adverse exchange rate movements. As a result, many treasurers take the view that forecast exposures, based on reasonable assumptions about future trading activity, should be treated as currency risks and managed accordingly. Exposure should therefore be considered to include both committed and uncommitted currency receipts and payments.

The examples of different types of exposure given above encompass two categories of exposure: translation and transaction exposure. These are the most commonly understood and recognized forms of currency exposure. A third kind – economic (also known as 'strategic', 'operational' or 'competitive') exposure – also occurs, but is less easy to quantify and manage and, indeed, although it is generally recognized to be a risk is largely left unmanaged by most corporates.

Translation exposure

Translation (or 'balance sheet') exposure can be defined as the risk that, when translated at the foreign exchange rates which will apply at a future balance sheet date will alter the domestic (or base) currency values of assets and liabilities in the balance sheet, resulting in a reported gain or loss.

Example of translation exposure A US company has a subsidiary in Germany that uses its local currency (the Deutsche Mark) as its functional currency. The subsidiary's balance sheet is translated into Dollars at the exchange rate ruling on the balance sheet date. Exchange rate movements from one balance sheet date to the next produce a period-to-period difference in the Dollar value of the German subsidiary's balance sheet.

	Net assets	Exchange rate	Dollar equivalent
Year 1	DEM 20 400 000	DEM 1.70	$12 000 000
Year 2	DEM 20 400 000	DEM 1.49	$13 691 275
Year 3	DEM 20 400 000	DEM 1.52	$13 421 052

The rates shown in the above example are the actual year end rates for the years 1989–1991. The example shows that, while there was no change in the DEM value of the net assets, the Dollar value fluctuated significantly as a result of exchange rate movements.

There is a great deal of debate about whether translation exposure really matters; some consider that it does not because its effect is simply on book values and not on cash flow. Those who believe that it does matter point to the effect that translation exposure can have on debt and reserves, and thus on gearing and, in turn, on compliance with covenants.

Those who argue against hedging translation exposure claim that the balance sheet value of an asset may, in any case, be questionable. It may be based on historical costs and been affected by such essentially subjective factors as revaluations, provisions, goodwill accounting, and so on, to the point at which the asset value, as a basis for hedging, is meaningless. Those in favour of hedging would counter this argument by pointing out that, despite these faults, the asset value in the balance sheet is, none the less, the accounting figure and as such should be hedged.

An argument against hedging, where the hedge takes the form of a liability created to match an asset in the same currency, is that the revaluation of the liability gives rise to a real change in the group's reported cash position. For example, net cash would be reduced in Sterling terms if the US Dollar strengthened and Dollar loans had been taken out to hedge Dollar assets. In this case, there has been a reduction in real cash in order to hedge an exposure that does not result in a cash outflow.

A company should also consider what the objectives of shareholders might be. Shareholders domiciled in different countries are likely to take differing views on the importance of translation exposure. For example, a US investor in a British, Sterling-based, company would see the Dollar value of its Sterling earnings reduce if the Dollar strengthened. From the US investor's point of view earnings per share will have fallen in Dollar terms. A British investor in the same company, on the other hand, would see the Sterling value of its Dollar earnings increase and a consequent rise in earnings per share.

The hedging policy undertaken by the company (and this may range anywhere between no hedging to being fully hedged) should take into account the effect on shareholders. In simple terms, an extreme policy of either no hedging or full hedging will, in the event of a continuing trend in the exchange rate in one direction, benefit one group of shareholders at the expense of the other group.

Some companies consider that the most equitable way to manage the exposure in such circumstances is to hedge in proportion to the company's overseas shareholder base. The question remains, however, as to the extent that shareholders deliberately invest in overseas companies to expose themselves to a range of currencies with the objective of spreading their risk. If this is a shareholder's strategy, it may well be defeated by the company hedging its translation exposure. For this reason, it is not unusual for a company that is contemplating a major translation hedging action that would substantially affect shareholder value to consult its main institutional shareholders before putting a hedge in place.

The hedging policy should take into account the effect onshareholders.

Transaction exposure

Transaction exposure can be defined as the risk that the base-currency value of a foreign-currency-denominated trading transaction will vary as a result of changes in exchange rates during the life of the trading transaction.

A typical example of a transaction exposure is the case of a company which incurs its costs, and accounts, in Sterling and buys components that are priced in foreign currency. The rate at which the company can purchase its foreign currency payables against Sterling will determine the level of profit that it makes on the sale. A strengthening of the foreign currency against Sterling will increase the Sterling cost and have a direct impact on profit. This is shown in the example below.

Example

➤ **A UK company buys components from a German supplier on 30-day payment terms – the goods are priced in Deutsche Marks.**

Price to UK company	DEM 1 000 000.00
Exchange rate at order date	DEM 2.30 = £1
Expected Sterling cost	£434 782.60

The company does not hedge the DEM payable and buys the DEM with a spot transaction against a sale of Sterling for value on the due date for payment.

Exchange rate on payment date	DEM 2.26 = £1
Actual Sterling cost	£442 477.87
Exchange loss	£7 695.27

The purchaser will have to decide how much, if any, of the increase in cost he can pass on to his customers through a price increase and how much he can afford to erode his own profit margins. Key factors in this decision will be elasticity of demand, the company's own financial strength and competitive pressures.

A seller of goods priced in a foreign currency is also exposed to the risk that his own currency will strengthen against the foreign currency and thereby reduce the proceeds of the sale in domestic currency terms. These goods may be raw materials, components, finished merchandise or services (the so-called 'invisibles').

An exporter whose base currency weakens on a consistent basis over time against the currency of its customers will enjoy a competitive advantage (see below) as the price of its goods and services to overseas customers will fall.

When does transaction exposure arise?

The point at which an organization can create a transaction exposure will vary according to its particular operating environment. Exposure can be created at each of the following events.

When a company issues a foreign-currency-denominated price list, it immediately exposes itself to the possibility of receiving currency revenues based on those prices and the risk that it will not be able to convert such revenues into its base currency at a rate that will result in the required profit margin.

When a currency denominated price list is issued

Clearly, if the company only hedges firm orders, it will be exposed to movements in exchange rates between the date that the price list is issued and the time that a firm order is received. In such circumstances it is common practice to hedge a proportion of the estimated sales volumes for the period in which the price list is in force.

An order from a customer would normally represent a clear commitment to pay at a future date and the point at which an order is agreed is commonly taken as the point at which a company selling in a foreign currency incurs an exposure.

When an order from a customer is accepted

In practice, however, there can be a number of complicating factors that should be considered when basing hedging decisions on the receipt of an order.

Is an oral order a commitment or should it be confirmed in writing? The delay involved in getting a documented order may be important if exchange rates are volatile and hedging will only take place on the basis of a signed order form. In such cases it will be necessary to agree with the customer the point at which (oral or written order) the price becomes binding upon each party.

Is the volume or quantity of the order fixed or is it simply an indication of the maximum amount that the purchaser may wish to buy? If there is scope for the purchaser to reduce the amount ordered, or to cancel the order completely, the company will have to assess the likelihood that the value of the order may be reduced and reduce the level of its hedging, or perhaps use currency options, to cater for this.

A firm order to purchase goods or services priced in foreign currency creates an exposure to the currency. While many companies would not hedge the exposure until the order, price and delivery date have been confirmed by the supplier, others would take the view that the exposure arises as soon as the order is placed and hedging should then be carried out without delay to protect against an adverse movement in exchange rates.

When a firm order to purchase goods or services is placed

When an
irrevocable tender is
submitted
A tender creates a contingent currency exposure. Because the exposure will only become a commitment if the tender is accepted, it would not be wise for the tenderer to enter into a binding foreign exchange transaction but it would be equally unwise to remain completely exposed to exchange movements.

Most companies that issue foreign-currency-denominated tenders therefore either include price escalation clauses in their tenders or hedge their contingent exposure by taking out option-based tenders to contract cover. These instruments are discussed in more detail in Chapter 5.

When a cross-
border funds
movement is made
Cross-border funds movements between group companies can take place for a variety of reasons apart from intercompany trading. Such movements include intercompany loans, dividend payments, capital contributions and management charges, most of which will be occasional or 'one-off' events. Because the amount and timing of such currency flows are fully under the control of the company, it is usually a straightforward matter for it to identify the optimum time to hedge the resulting exposures and it is not uncommon to find that hedging action is taken well in advance of the actual movement of funds.

> *A tender creates a contingent currency exposure.*

Economic exposure

Economic exposure arises in a number of ways; each of which derives from the position of a company in relation to its competitors. Economic exposure may be direct or indirect, as illustrated by the following examples.

**Direct economic
exposure**
A UK company exports to Belgium and prices in Belgian Francs. It is competing against Belgian companies who, of course, also price in Belgian Francs but who have Belgian Franc costs. The UK company has Sterling costs and will suffer a competitive disadvantage if Sterling strengthens against the Belgian Franc. If Sterling does strengthen, the UK company will suffer a reduction in its Sterling proceeds if it maintains its Belgian Franc prices. If it puts its prices up to maintain its profit margin, it may lose market share and, in turn, still suffer some loss of profit.

Indirect exposure can arise in a variety of ways. For example, a US company is exporting to an overseas market in competition with another US company. It hedges its foreign currency receipts into Dollars to lock in its Dollar income at a level that will give it a satisfactory profit margin. Its competitor has not hedged its currency receipts, as it expects the Dollar to weaken. If the Dollar does depreciate, the competitor will be able to reduce its local currency prices and gain market share at the expense of its rival, or maintain its prices and benefit from the increased strength of the foreign currency against the Dollar.

Indirect economic exposure

Indirect exposure also occurs when suppliers based in different countries are competing for sales in another country. For example, British and German motor manufacturers are competing in the French market. The British manufacturer will be exposed not just to the Sterling/French Franc exchange rate but also to the relative movements in the Deutsche Mark/French Franc rate. All other things being equal, the British manufacturer will gain a competitive advantage if Sterling weakens against the French Franc to a greater extent than the Deutsche Mark does.

Economic exposure, therefore, comprises a range of factors: the geographical locations in which a company is based and incurs costs, the locations of its competitors, the hedging strategies of its competitors and the differential movements in exchange rates. Some of these factors a company can control; it may, for example, establish manufacturing operations in key markets. Other factors, such as the hedging strategies adopted by competitors, may be unquantifiable and, if they are known, may not be considered appropriate.

It is doubtful whether a company could ever accurately assess its economic exposure (most have difficulty in forecasting transaction exposure) and, if it could, it would still have to second guess the analytical expertise and strategies of its competitors. However, companies should attempt to identify key elements of their economic exposure and perform simple scenario analyses to ascertain their tolerance to major exchange rate movements.

The above are definitions of the types of exposure to which it is possible to be exposed; identifying these is only, however, the first step in understanding and managing currency risk. There are a number of further steps that every organization should take *before dealing in the currency markets* which are essential to the effective and efficient management of currency risk. Dealing should be seen as the end of a process that disposes of the residue of exposure that is left after other exposure management techniques (such as pricing mechanisms, leading and lagging and netting) have been employed. The more effectively these other techniques are used, the fewer foreign exchange transactions will be required, and the lower the cost of managing the exposures is likely to be.

Forecasting currency exposure

The approach to forecasting currency exposure will vary according to the type of exposure involved. As we discussed above, translation exposure affects the balance sheet and is forecast through the construction of projected balance sheets. Transaction exposure, on the other hand, affects the profit and loss account and is forecast by means of a currency cash flow forecast. Economic exposure, insofar as it is possible to forecast it (and few corporations do), is likely to emerge from long-term plans and reviews covering periods up to ten years ahead.

> *Transaction exposure affects the profit and loss account.*

The discussion about forecasting methods that follows refers to exposures that will, or are expected to, crystallize at some future date. As far as transaction exposures are concerned therefore, an exposure forecast will include both 'committed' currency receipts and payments (arising from firm sales and orders and usually represented as debtor and creditor items in the accounts) which will be paid or received within the corporation's standard payment periods, and 'uncommitted' exposures that are projections based on reasonable assumptions about continuing business patterns.

Forecasting translation exposure

Translation exposure is forecast by using a balance sheet basis source and application of funds projection to produce a projected balance sheet by currency.

The forecast takes as its starting point the actual position at a past balance sheet date, which is typically the last year end or half year position. Changes to the balance sheet items that will take place during the next period are then calculated. These changes will either be known in advance or based on agreed assumptions. Known changes, for example, might include committed capital investment, acquisitions and divestments that will be reflected as changes in fixed assets or equity investments. Projected changes, for example in working capital, might reflect changes in payment and credit terms or in inventory turn rates. In addition, there will be assumptions about profit, and tax and dividend payments. The projected balance sheet is the product of the opening balance sheet plus the projected changes.

It will be apparent that some elements of the forecast balance sheet, such as debtors, short-term creditors and stocks, are items that arise as a result of ongoing trading activity. Currency exposures on these balance sheet items are, as discussed above, classified and treated as transaction exposures rather than translation exposures. If we eliminate these, and other short-term items such as dividend payments from subsidiaries to the parent company, which are also treated as transaction exposures, we are left with a core of long-term (and usually significant) balance sheet items on which any translation exposure will be incurred. These items include currency denominated fixed assets, debt, and long-term cash surpluses. The extent to which there is an imbalance in the values of these items by currency is the measure of the company's balance sheet exposure.

A simple example of the way in which a company can incur and forecast translation exposure is described below.

GB Manufacturing Limited is a British company with a German branch that has a factory manufacturing components for the motor industry. GB Manufacturing owns the factory buildings and the machinery and financed their purchase through Sterling debt. The balance sheet entries relating to the fixed asset investment are shown below. (In reality, the balance sheets would, of course, be far more complex than those shown below. In the example we are concentrating on just two elements within the overall balance sheet.)

Year 1 (millions)	GBP	DEM
Fixed assets		100.0
Debt	(40.0)	
Net	(40.0)	100.0

During Year 2 GB Manufacturing purchases machinery from a German supplier for DEM 2 million. The purchase, at an exchange rate of DEM 2.40 = £1, cost £833 000, and is again funded by Sterling borrowing. The balance sheet at the end of Year 2 is therefore projected at:

Year 2 (millions)	GBP	DEM
Fixed assets		102.0
Debt	(40.8)	
Net	(40.8)	102.0

GB Manufacturing are therefore able to forecast that their translation exposure to the Deutsche Mark will be DEM 102 million at end of the current year; an increase of DEM 2 million compared with the previous year end.

In the above example, GB Manufacturing's exposure to the Deutsche Mark increased by DEM 2 million because its acquisition of Deutsche Mark-denominated assets was financed by non-Deutsche Mark debt. If the machinery had been financed by local borrowings in Deutsche Marks the balance sheets would have appeared as follows:

Year 2 (millions)	GBP	DEM
Fixed assets		102.0
Debt	(40.0)	(2.0)
Net	(40.0)	100.0

In this case, the Deutsche Mark-denominated asset is matched by a Deutsche Mark-denominated liability and there is no net change in the currency exposure. This very simple example illustrates how a company can identify changes to its translation exposure (by adjusting a known position for actual and expected changes) and also manage that exposure by the currency it uses to fund its assets.

Companies with more complex translation exposures – across a range of currencies and balance sheet items – often use computer models to produce balance sheet forecasts. In essence, the models work in the same way as our simple example; they adjust a known starting point for the effects of both contracted and expected changes in balance sheet items.

Forecasting transaction exposure

The basic tool for forecasting transaction exposures is a currency cash flow forecast. Transaction exposures will arise when any of the following actions are denominated in a foreign currency:

- sales to customers
- purchases of raw materials, components, services and fuel
- purchases of finished goods
- purchase and sale of capital equipment
- acquisitions, disposals and divestments, and
- receipts and payments of interest and dividends.

The amounts, currencies and timings of these flows will typically originate from such projections as sales and production budgets and forecasts, capital investment plans, and treasury investment and borrowing data. Underlying these budgets and forecasts there will be assumptions for each country in which the company operates about the size of the market,

> *The basic tool for forecasting transaction exposures is a currency cash flow forecast.*

the company's market share by product line, pricing decisions, materials sourcing decisions, production cycles and changes in the levels of working capital. These will then be consolidated to produce group cash flow forecasts by currency. These forecasts will be complex and interrelated calculations that link the operating cost bases and revenue streams with non-operational flows such as capital expenditure, dividends, interest and other 'one-off' flows.

It is essential that the cash flow forecasts are internally consistent if they are to be a reliable basis for managing exposure. Clearly, if raw materials or components are purchased for use in the production process, and eventual sale as finished goods, the volumes of materials purchased must be related to the volumes of both production and sales (with any differences explained by a change in the levels of stocks) and the timing of the flows of expected payments and receipts should also relate to recognized production, sales and payment cycles.

Economic exposure is the hardest kind of exposure to forecast. Strictly speaking, an attempt at forecasting should not be aimed at economic exposure itself, which is a qualitative rather than a quantitative risk, but at the effects of economic exposure. **Forecasting economic exposure**

These effects will be seen in terms of the changes that will occur over time – principally in profitability and market share – as a result of changes in the company's competitive position. They can be identified using computer models that use broad assumptions about exchange rates, market sizes, competition, pricing, inflation and so on. The chief difficulty in quantifying economic exposure is that because so many factors can affect a projection of future profitability, particularly in a highly competitive market with many participants, it is difficult, if not impossible, to isolate the effects of exchange rates alone.

Some corporates, operating in industries where there a few competitors and a dominant currency (and in which it is possible to take a long-term view), such as the oil and aerospace industries, are better able than most to identify economic risk, albeit only in very broad terms. This is often expressed simply in terms of an exchange rate below which the company will no longer be able to remain profitable, as in 'If the Dollar strengthens to $1.30, we will go out of business'. In such circumstances, a major preoccupation of the treasury will be in hedging its main currency risks out into the future to ensure that the 'survival' exchange rate is bettered.

Forecasting exchange rates

Corporations that go to the trouble of forecasting their currency exposures will naturally want to put those forecasts into the context of their expectations for exchange rate movements. In large multinational companies, it is common to find that exchange rate forecasts are produced in-house by the companies' economists, planners or the treasury department. Where there are no in-house forecasting resources, companies generally rely on exchange rate projections and market commentary provided by their relationship banks.

The theory and practice of exchange rate forecasting is a story of two distinct approaches. Economists use forecasts of economic fundamentals to make longer-term forecasts while technical analysts base their short-term predictions on the experience of pricing history in the market. While each of these approaches has its shortcomings, each also has a valuable contribution to make towards increasing the understanding of the forces that influence exchange rate movements over both the short and the long term.

Using statistical models

In Chapter 1 we discussed the economic factors that influence exchange rates over the longer term. It would seem reasonable that, if we can identify why exchange rates move, we should be able to make an acceptable forecast of future exchange rates based on projections of the factors that influence them. This approach is indeed the traditional method for forecasting exchange rates. Economists construct statistical models which incorporate all of the factors that are relevant to the currency to be forecast (the 'endogenous variables') and apply a weighting to these factors based on historical data. As we know, exchange rates are also influenced by political and psychological factors. The effect of these 'exogenous variables' must also be built into the model in order to simulate realistic conditions.

Comparisons between the rates forecast by such models and the actual outturn in the market, however, reveal that the models tend to be inaccurate. This could be explained by errors in forecasting the exogenous variables, but detailed analysis indicates that errors in this area have little effect on the accuracy of a forecast. It seems likely that the main reason for the failure of models to produce accurate forecasts is that the historical weighting of all of the factors that influence exchange rates is no guide to the future relationship of these factors. A forecaster could therefore, estimate accurately all of the relevant factors but still produce an inaccurate exchange rate projection because the wrong weighting had been applied to each factor.

Market expectations

The failure of models as a reliable basis for projecting future exchange rates prompted market practitioners to seek other explanations for movements in prices. Attention turned to the link between price movements and the market's expectations. It was suggested that, if an individual had strong enough grounds for believing that the price of a financial asset would rise in the future, that individual would buy the asset now so as to benefit from the rise in its value. (The theory also, of course, works in reverse, with assets being sold in the expectation of a future fall in the price.) If a sufficient number of people took the same view, they would also act in the same way and the price of the asset would rise (or fall) until the current price was equal to the expected future price, adjusted for any costs (such as interest) incurred by carrying the asset. At that point the spot price would reflect the market's expectation of its future value. A spot foreign exchange rate would thus, after adjustment for any interest differential, reflect the expected future rate. This view, that the spot rate is the discounted present value of a future forward rate, reverses the orthodox view of the forward rate being the adjusted price of the current spot rate.

This approach to explaining future prices is supported by two theories.

The theory of rational expectations
·····················

This theory assumes that people learn from their experiences and avoid repeating mistakes. In the forecasting context, this means that forecasters will constantly refine their projections in an attempt to eliminate errors. While this cannot guarantee that a forecast will be correct, it will at least exclude any identified areas of inaccuracy.

The efficient market hypothesis
·····················

This hypothesis relates to the information on which forecasts are based. It states that all available information is fully reflected in the price of an asset (or, less strongly, that all publicly available information is reflected in the price). In its weakest form, the hypothesis states that the best forecast of a future price of an asset is the current price; after adjusting, as noted above, for carrying costs, such as interest rates.

> The theory of rational expectations assumes that people learn from their experiences.

In essence, the hypothesis holds that there is no better forecast of the future price of an asset than its interest-adjusted spot price. This view, in disregarding the previous price history of the asset in favour of the current price, contradicts the assumptions implicit in techniques based upon historical price movements. (These techniques, which are discussed later in this chapter, have in recent years become significant in the quantification of risk.)

The view that the current price of an asset incorporates all presently known information and thus reflects future expectations leads to the conclusion that, if current expectations prove to be correct, there will be no change in the price of the asset. Or, more accurately, the price will rise over time to take into account carrying costs and a return which reflects the risk in holding the asset. The practical difficulty with the theory is that the future almost never turns out as expected, particularly over the longer term. Unexpected events (which, by definition, are not reflected in the price) therefore cause a change in the price. These unexpected events occur as random shocks and should be reflected over time as random movements (volatility) in the price of an asset. Depending upon the asset in question, this 'random walk' may occur around a long-term trend.

> The efficient market hypothesis holds that the best forecast of a future price is its interest-adjusted spot price.

These theories leave forecasters of exchange rates in a difficult position. The spot rate already reflects future expectations based on a certain set of rational expectations, such as economic forecasts. If those expectations are proved by events to be correct the rate should not change (or will change only to the extent justified by the interest rate differential). If they are not correct, it will be because unexpected events – random shocks – have intervened to cause the spot rate to change. Since it is not possible to forecast unexpected events there is no better information available about future rates at any point in time than the current market rates. On this basis, the forecaster is out of a job.

Economic fundamentals, despite their shortcomings, are still the basis for longer-term exchange rate forecasts. Many operators in the market, however, are more interested in the outlook for a short term that is measured in days, rather than months, and for which economic data are not relevant. These operators, who are chiefly banks but who also include corporations, are interested in how the market is expected to move today or this week as they need to decide the precise timing of a transaction and wish to act in the market at the most favourable moment. The information they require to assist them in timing their hedging actions is provided by technical analysts, or 'chartists' as they are often called.

Technical analysis

Chartists act on the belief that the economic fundamentals are already recognized by the market and reflected in current prices and that they have therefore been 'discounted' by the market. Their forecast of prices is based on 'technical' information that has been generated by the market, such as prices and the volume of trading. Chartists study the long-term price patterns in the market and use these as the basis for predicting short-term price movements. While economists regard the chartists' techniques and results with scepticism, traders in the market take their predictions seriously and act upon them. Because of this, the forecasts of the chartists tend to become self-fulfilling as the market is prompted to react when rates reach key 'chart points'.

> *Chartists act on the belief that the economic fundamentals are reflected in current prices and have therefore been 'discounted' by the market.*

Chartists recognize certain patterns in price history and use these patterns to predict movements in rates over the very short term. The key patterns include the following

Head and shoulders

This pattern is formed by a major rise (the head) which separates two smaller rises (the shoulders). When this pattern is developing, the price is expected to fall to a point level with the bottom of the first shoulder.

Broadening top
This pattern displays three peaks reaching successively higher levels. Between each peak is a bottom, the second of which is lower than the first. If the price falls after the third peak to a level below the second bottom, a major reversal in the trend is indicated.

Double bottoms/tops
A double bottom or top points to a major reversal in the price trend. The double bottom or top consists of two troughs or peaks separated by a movement in the opposite direction.

Momentum models and moving averages
In addition to studying pricing patterns, technical analysts also use momentum and moving average models. Momentum models analyze the rate of change in price movements rather than the movements themselves. An increase in the rate of change is taken to indicate that a trend will continue, while a decrease in the rate indicates an imminent reversal in the trend. The theory behind moving averages is that pricing trends can be predicted by analysing short and long-term moving average prices; a major change is expected when a long-term moving average crosses a short-term moving average.

The reader would be quite justified at this point in feeling some despair about the prospects for the development of a reliable method of exchange rate forecasting. This despair could only deepen when it is appreciated that surveys of the accuracy of foreign exchange forecasts tend to show that they are wrong more often than they are right. In such circumstances, the currency exposure manager is perhaps wise to canvass as wide a range of opinion as possible, and then form his own view.

> *Momentum models analyze the rate of change in price movements.*

Quantifying currency risk

There are a number of different techniques that treasurers use to quantify the amount of *risk* that corporations face. It is important to recognize that the risk is the effect on the profit and loss account or the balance sheet that would result from a movement in exchange rates. As such, it will normally be a small proportion of the absolute exposure level because exchange rates, even at times of great volatility, tend to move within relatively narrow limits over the very short term.

Thus, a 15 cent (10 per cent) depreciation in Sterling against the Dollar from $1.50 to $1.35, while appearing to be a dramatic movement, would be likely to take place over at least a couple of days. This will give an alert corporate the opportunity to put cover in place before the full extent of the movement has occurred. In this case, the maximum risk to a company may have been 10 per cent of its unhedged short Dollar position, but it may have hedged quickly and put cover in place to limit its loss to 5 per cent or even less.

The elements of risk quantification therefore, are:

● absolute exposure level

multiplied by

● exchange movement expressed in percentage or 'rate' terms

equals risk.

Given that the exposure level has already been calculated, and is not in dispute, the key element in this calculation is the amount of the exchange rate movement that is applied to the exposure to calculate the level of risk. There are a variety of approaches used in quantifying exchange risk. The most commonly used (or at least commonly discussed) are described below.

A scenario analysis simply takes the current levels of exposure (i.e. unhedged currency positions) and translates them into the base currency at both current market rates and forecast exchange rates. (For the purposes of the exercise, one would normally assume that forecast exchange rates were different from those available in the market. This, of course, implies a rejection of the efficient market hypothesis: that the forward rate is a forecast of the future spot rate.)

Scenario analysis based on exchange rate forecasts

A simple example of this method of risk evaluation is set out below.

Currency	Month 1	Month 2	Month 3
Deutsche Marks	(8 000 000.00)	(6 000 000.00)	(9 000 000.00)
Current market rates	2.2450	2.2400	2.2350
Sterling equivalent	3 563 474.30	2 678 571.40	4 026 845.60
Forecast spot rates	2.2300	2.2300	2.2200
Sterling equivalent	3 587 443.90	2 690 582.90	4 054 054.00
Exchange risk	(23 969.60)	(12 011.50)	(27 208.40)

This simple analysis shows:

● the exposure – short positions in Deutsche Marks arising, for example, from purchases of raw materials from a German supplier

- the current market rates at which those exposures can be hedged in the forward market and the Sterling cost of doing so
- the company's own forecast for spot Deutsche Mark against Sterling for the relevant time periods and the Sterling cost of Deutsche Marks at these rates, and
- the foreign exchange 'loss' that would result if the company did not hedge and bought spot at the forecast rates. These amounts represent the risk to the company of not hedging.

A basic problem with this method of risk quantification lies in the selection of the forecast exchange rates. Clearly, the forecast rates should be based on reasonable expectations derived from economic and other (e.g. political) data. The resulting rates may, however, be proved in the event to have been wildly wrong but, in the meantime, have been used to make hedging decisions. This is a particular problem when, because a favourable movement in rates is forecast, an exposure is left unhedged. Running an exposed position is generally regarded as speculative. Immediate hedging of an exposure on the other hand, (even if done at rates that could subsequently have been bettered), is usually regarded as prudent and risk averse.

> *Running an exposed position is generally regarded as speculative.*

Effect of 1 per cent movement/1 cent movement
....

Another way of looking at exchange rate risk is to quantify it in terms of the effect on profits of a movement of 1 per cent in the exchange rate or of a particular amount, such as 1 US cent or some other appropriate amount in a relevant currency.

Thus a British manufacturer with a significant exposure to the US Dollar may be able to quantify the effect on profit of both a strengthening or weakening of the Dollar. This is likely not to be simply a matter of calculating the change in the cost in Sterling of raw materials or the value of Dollar revenues. An estimate will normally be made of the extent to which any increased costs can be passed on to the customer through price increases or will be absorbed. Similarly, where revenue is in a foreign currency, a strengthening of the currency might result in a reduction in currency prices (and increased market share), a higher base currency unit profit or a combination of the two. On the other hand, a company might respond to a weakening of the currency by maintaining existing prices in the hope that increased sales will offset lower unit profits or, to the extent that it is commercially possible, increasing its prices to maintain the level of its revenue in base currency terms. In cases where a variety of responses may be made by the company to a movement in exchange rates, it is common practice to use a computer model to determine the optimum balance between changing prices and improving market share.

Assuming that all these considerations have been factored into the calculation, it should be possible to arrive at a 'rule of thumb' measurement of the effect of a movement in exchange rates for any given volume of sales or materials' purchases. The following example, of a company with US Dollar payables, illustrates the way in which the exchange rate risk is quantified.

Exposure amount	$(10 000 000.00)
Current exchange rate vs Sterling	$1.5000
Sterling value at current rate	$6 666 666.66
Value of 1% rate movement	1.50 cents
Exchange rate after 1% movement	$1.4850
Sterling value	£6 734 006.70
Profit effect of 1% movement in rate	£(67 340.04)

The example shows that a *strengthening* of the US Dollar by 1 per cent from $1.5000 to $1.4850 increases the Sterling value of $10 million by £67 340.04. A company receiving US Dollar revenue would benefit, and a company paying a supplier would suffer an increase in costs, by this amount. It is important to note, however, that a weakening of the Dollar by 1 per cent has a slightly different profit effect.

If the Dollar had *weakened* by 1 per cent from $1.5000 to $1.5150 the Sterling value of $10 000 000.00 would have been £6 600 660.00. Compared with a Sterling value of £6 666 666.66 at a rate of $1.50, this is a change of £66 006.66.

The calculation of the effect of a 1 US cent movement (or a similar movement in a different currency) is performed in the same way as for the 1 per cent movement, as shown in the example below. In this example, a company has US Dollar payables and is therefore exposed to a strengthening of the Dollar.

Exposure amount	$(10 000 000.00)
Current exchange rate	$1.5000
Sterling value at current rate	£6 666 666.66
Exchange rate after 1 cent movement	$1.4900
Sterling value	£6 711 409.30
Effect of 1 cent movement	£(44 742.64)

Once the effects of percentage or absolute rate movements are known, they can be used as a rough 'ready reckoner'. Thus, in the first example, the company will know that a 5 per cent movement in Sterling against the Dollar will result in a profit effect of about a third of a million pounds. In the second example, a 5 cent movement is worth £224 000. Quantification of the effects of exchange rate movements in terms of their effect on profits in this way is an essential element of the risk management process.

Stress testing

Stress testing is a logical extension of the analysis discussed above. In essence, all it attempts to do is put limits on the ability to survive exchange rate movements. In analysing the effect of percentage and absolute movements in exchange rates we were able to quantify the effects of those movements on profits. While we could then say what the effect on profits might be, this did not tell us whether we would still be in business. We need, therefore, to be able to put extreme exchange rate movements into the context of viability of the business. Stress tests aim to assess the effects of sudden and abnormally large market movements of the kind that affected Sterling when it was suspended from the ERM in October 1992 and immediately fell dramatically on the foreign exchange markets.

Stress testing is perhaps best performed using a currency cash flow forecast model in which extreme exchange rate movements and their effects on pricing, materials sourcing and sales can be measured. This kind of analysis has a number of benefits: if it is performed in collaboration with marketing and production staff (who are very often the people responsible for creating currency exposures in the first place) it demonstrates to them the need to consider the foreign exchange risk implications of their actions; it enables the company to consider and plan what actions they can take in the event of an extreme rate movement (for example, the extent to which it can be reflected in pricing and alternative sources of materials and components); and it provides the 'rule of thumb' exchange rate below which the company is no longer able to survive against the competition of overseas companies in the same industry.

Value at Risk (VaR)

At the time of writing there is much interest among corporate treasurers in the concept of 'Value at Risk' for measuring foreign exchange risk. This methodology, which is widely used by banks and financial institutions, uses a statistical analysis of past volatility in rates to assess the level of risk to which a position or a portfolio is exposed. An exposed currency position could be composed of both transaction exposures from future revenue streams and translation exposures from currency-denominated assets and liabilities in the balance sheet.

There are two key elements in using Value at Risk as a risk measurement technique: the assessment of risk for a single currency and the understanding of the relationships (or 'correlation coefficients') between currencies that enable risk to be reduced by diversification across a range of currencies.

Using historical rates to predict future risk has been likened to steering one's car by looking in the rear view mirror.

If we accept that the risk in holding a currency exposure (rather than hedging it with, for example, a forward contract) is that the eventual conversion rate will be different from the current forward rate, we can begin to measure the uncertainty that arises in holding an open position. This could be done (laboriously) by analyzing all the possible outcomes, and the probability of each outcome occurring, using Monte Carlo analysis. Or, with less effort, using standard deviation to summarize the spread of possible outcomes, based on historical data. Value at Risk, as a risk management technique, is based on the premise that currency risk can be measured as the standard deviation of expected returns, provided that those returns are normally distributed.

As, for this purpose, currency returns are assumed to be zero (that is, interest plus exchange movement in one currency over time equals interest plus exchange movement in any other freely traded currency), the only information that is needed to model currency risk is the volatility or standard deviation of the currency. These data must, of necessity, be historical. (It is on this point that the debate about the Value at Risk as a risk management technique hinges. History is not necessarily an accurate guide to the future; the period covered by the historical data may contain random shocks or other temporary distortions. Using historical rates to predict future risk has been likened by some critics to 'steering one's car by looking in the rear view mirror').

Value at Risk is expressed as a measure of risk-adjusted potential loss. If a company calculates that it has a VaR of $5 million using a 30-day holding period with 95 per cent probability, this means that 95 per cent of the time the company will lose less than $5 million over 30 days and in only 5 per cent of the time will it lose more than $5 million. What VaR does not tell it is how much more than $5 million it might lose in the 5 per cent of the time. Neither does it tell it how much will be lost 95 per cent of the time; the $5 million is simply an upper limit.

A company that is considering using Value at Risk as a risk management tool will need to consider the following points.

- Historical rate data are required to perform the calculation and those data have to be consistent with conditions in the future period that is under consideration. Thus the data for a currency that had just been freed from exchange controls would not be suitable for use in a Value at Risk calculation until a period of free market trading had elapsed.

- It may be possible to calculate a Value at Risk number from historical data but not be possible to hedge the risk because of regulatory restrictions or market incapacity. Under these conditions it may be considered futile to calculate the VaR figure.

- What is an appropriate future period to look ahead? The longer the period, the greater both the price and (probably) the Value at Risk will be. A company may decide that it should only calculate the Value at Risk on committed currency flows covering, say, the next three months.

- What confidence level should be chosen? In our example above, the 95 per cent confidence level implied that 1 time in 20 the loss will exceed the $5 million Value at Risk. A 98 per cent confidence level, on the other hand, means that only 1 time in 50 would the loss exceed $5 million. Most companies are likely to take a prudent approach and set a high confidence level.

Correlation An understanding of how movements in currencies correlate, or do not correlate, assists the management of currency risk. We can develop the principles established in analyzing Value at Risk to cover a range of currencies. Portfolio theory holds that the relationship between the returns from one currency and another is as important as each currency's individual risk and return. Relationships between currencies are usually expressed in terms of their correlation coefficients.

These can be summarized as follows:

- Currencies that have *positive correlation* move in the same direction.
- Currencies that have *negative correlation* move in opposite directions.
- Where there is *no correlation* each currency moves independently.

The correlation coefficient is expressed as a value between minus one and plus one. A coefficient of one means that the two currencies are perfectly correlated (they will move the same amount in the same direction), while a correlation coefficient of less than one means that risk is reduced by holding the two currencies in a portfolio. Perfectly negatively correlated currencies form a perfect hedge (so long as the amounts are equal). It should be understood, however, that in attempting to construct hedges through negative correlation the company may be exposed if its financial data are inaccurate or if future market correlations differ from historical patterns. The risk that can be eliminated by holding a diverse portfolio is termed 'unique' or 'specific' risk. There is, however, some risk that cannot be avoided or eliminated through diversification; this risk is called 'market' risk.

To calculate the risk for a portfolio of different currencies requires data for the volatility of the currencies and their correlation coefficients. While it is comparatively easy to calculate the risk for a two-currency portfolio, it is much more complicated when more currencies are involved and a computer system is generally needed.

The ultimate objective of using correlation coefficients in currency risk management is to be able to recognize the effect on risk of diversification and to be able to use this knowledge in the management of exposure.

Summary

We have aimed in this chapter to set out some important principles for identifying and understanding the nature of currency risk. These are summarized below.

- Every organization needs to understand the nature of the currency exposure that it faces, how that exposure is incurred and the amounts, timings and currencies of which it is composed.

- The need for an organization both to understand the long and short-term influences on exchange rates and to be able to form an opinion about future currency trends.

- The need to understand and be able to use the techniques for assessing the *risk* to the organization from unhedged exposures.

Why should an organization do all this? Stated simply, the understanding, identification and quantification of risk are the foundations for the currency exposure management process. They form the logical basis for determining the organization's attitude to risk and therefore its risk management policies, procedures, controls and organizational arrangements.

The foundation for the management of foreign exchange risk is a clearly defined policy and organizational framework.

Policies and organization

- The policy framework
- The organizational framework

The foundation for the effective, efficient and secure management of foreign exchange risk is an appropriate and clearly defined policy and organizational framework.

The policy framework

A statement of the organization's attitude to risk

The foreign exchange exposure management policy document should have specific features if it is to fulfil its purpose. The features typically include:

An organization's attitude to risk is likely to be based on a number of factors, which could include:

- the size and nature of the currency risks faced by the organization, as identified and quantified by the processes described in the previous chapter;

- the ability to change prices in response to fluctuating exchange rates. Where the effects of adverse exchange rate movements can be recovered by price increases without affecting sales volumes the organization will regard itself as largely insulated against exchange risk and may therefore be relatively indifferent to it;

- the nature of the other risks that the business faces. A company with uncontrollable non-financial risks may be highly risk averse with regard to currency exposure simply because this is one area that can be controlled. One example of this is a company in the agricultural sector that is strongly dependent on good weather;

- the approach taken by direct competitors in the same business or market sector. To the extent that they are known, the policies of competitors can influence other companies. A view is often taken that it is better to be in step with the opposition, even if that means that everyone is doing the wrong thing, rather than run the risk of being on one's own;

- the resources and skills available to the company in managing currency exposure. Active management of exposure demands a greater level of investment in people and systems (with no guaranteed benefit); many organizations adopt straightforward and risk averse policies simply because they are regarded as least expensive; and

- the personalities and experiences of the members of the Board. In many organizations, the personal financial fortunes of Board members will be at risk. In others, directors (particularly non-executive directors) may have personal experience of currency losses in other companies with which they have been associated or may simply be aware of a disaster in another company. These influences are likely to result in a risk averse stance even where currency may not be a major element in the company's operations.

The role of the treasury will be determined by the organization's attitude to risk. If the appetite for risk is strong, the treasury may well operate as a *profit centre*. The characteristics of a profit centre treasury are that it is allowed to trade and to take positions, which need not relate to the underlying business of the organization, with the objective of making profit. A profit centre treasury might, for example, sell a currency forward in the expectation that the currency will weaken and a profit can be made when the maturing forward sale is closed out with a spot purchase of the currency.

A description of the role of the treasury

Such trading and position taking is, of course, entirely speculative, and it is the speculative and optional (because it is not driven by any underlying commercial activity) nature of the profit centre treasury's activity that distinguishes it from *cost centre* and *value-added service centre* treasuries. Because profit centre treasuries engage in these additional and risky speculative activities, they generally require more staff and a greater degree of information and analytical and systems support than other types of treasury.

A *cost centre* treasury is usually found in an extremely risk-averse organization. Its role will be to eliminate exposure as soon as it is identified. Where the cost centre treasury deals on behalf of subsidiary companies it normally provides a simple deal execution service, arranging the transaction without delay and passing the rate obtained from the bank directly to the subsidiary. It does not seek to make a turn on the transaction or 'play the market' to obtain an advantageous rate. A cost centre treasury is unlikely to find itself responsible for a treasury disaster but could be incurring unidentified opportunity costs as a result of its essentially passive approach to exposure management.

> *If the appetite for risk is strong, the treasury may act as a profit centre.*

The *value-added service centre* treasury fits between the extremes of the profit and cost centre treasuries. Its objective is to add value through the active management of exposure within clearly defined parameters. It does not create new exposures for speculative purposes nor does it simply close out all exposures as soon as they are identified. Rather, it typically reduces the level of exposure by selective hedging and aims to manage the remaining unhedged balance so that any opportunities to benefit from expected movements in currency rates may be exploited. Where an organization operates a value-added service centre treasury the policies and controls must be particularly clearly stated and effectively implemented in order to prevent the treasury from behaving more as a profit centre treasury.

Because there are these different types of treasury role and because there is scope for wide interpretation of how each type of treasury could operate in practice, it is essential that a treasury policy statement should not simply state that the treasury should act as, for example, a value-added service centre, it should also define in as much detail as necessary what this means for the organization concerned. The process of definition will, incidentally, be valuable in clarifying practical details of how the treasury relates to subsidiaries and how it performs the dealing process.

How currency exposures are identified and reported The policies should define the types of exposure which the organization has (for example, translation exposure, and committed and forecast transaction exposures) and specify how each should be identified and reported. The identification and reporting process may well (rightly or wrongly) be determined by the organization's attitude to risk and the role of the treasury. Where a value-added service centre treasury is in operation there is typically more emphasis on forecasting than in the cost centre treasury where it is common to find that hedging is carried out only in respect of committed exposures.

Policies with regard to exposure forecasting and reporting should specify, as a minimum, the following requirements:

- the responsibility for forecasting and the recipient department
- the frequency of forecasting (for example, monthly on the fifth working day)
- the time horizon and reporting periods (for example, a rolling 12 months' forecast by month)
- the types of exposure to be forecast
- where appropriate, the basis for the forecast (for example, latest sales or production assumptions issued centrally), and
- a standard reporting format.

In some organizations, subsidiaries may be free to deal direct with banks, while in others all dealing will have to be through the group treasury. It is not uncommon, also, to find cases in which there is a mix of these two approaches, with small deals or those in certain currencies being arranged by subsidiaries directly with banks and other exposures being managed centrally. The policy statement must set out the authorities and process by which hedging is to be implemented.

Where hedging can be arranged by subsidiaries directly with banks, there must be a process by which such hedging can be controlled to ensure that it is carried out in conformity with exposure management policies and that counterparty risks and relationships are monitored and managed.

Where all dealing goes through the treasury, there will need to be a process by which formal and properly authorised requests for hedges are made by the subsidiaries to the treasury. There will also need to be agreed rules for the time period in which hedges must be executed and whether the treasury can charge the subsidiary a margin or not.

The policies with regard to dealing might also stipulate that deals over a certain size must be quoted competitively to at least two banks, that a particular process be followed for selecting the banks that are asked to quote, and that a sequentially numbered deal ticket be completed for each transaction. In addition, there must be policies that ensure that key control processes, such as segregation of duties and two-way confirmation or matching of transaction details, are in place and operate effectively.

There may be specified minimum and maximum levels of cover that must be taken in respect of given categories of exposure. This is likely to vary according to the role of the treasury: a profit centre treasury will normally have a completely free hand to hedge or not to hedge at its discretion (as well as to take positions in excess of 100 per cent of the exposure or where there is no underlying exposure). A cost centre treasury, on the other hand, will typically be expected to hedge its recognized exposures in full.

It is in the case of the value-added cost centre that it is most necessary to spell out in detail the levels of cover that must be taken if an appropriate degree of control is to be achieved. A balance has to be struck between allowing too much discretion (and running the risk of over exposure) and imposing too high a level of mandatory cover (and constraining unnecessarily the ability of the treasury to add value by the application of its expertise). Typically, the policies will require higher levels of cover for the near term, for which the forecast is likely to be more accurate and to include a high proportion of committed currency-denominated purchases and sales, and lower levels of cover for later time periods as the accuracy and certainty of the forecast diminishes.

Thus the policy may stipulate that exposures for the next three months must be fully hedged as currency flows in this period, based on 90-day payment terms, are considered to be commitments arising from firm orders and sales. For periods further out, lower minimum levels of cover may be set: for example, 75 per cent for 4–6 months; 50 per cent for 7–9 months and 25 per cent for 10–12 months. Figure 3.1 illustrates the exposure background against which a hedging policy may be formulated.

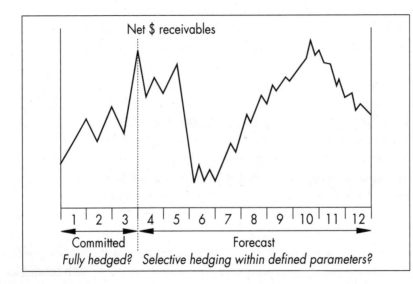

Figure 3.1

Establishing a hedging policy – what do you hedge?

Authorization to use particular hedging instruments It is standard practice for treasuries to use spot and forward foreign exchange contracts to manage currency exposure and many companies find that these instruments meet all their hedging needs. Increasingly, however, more sophisticated techniques involving the use of currency options or borrowings are being used to manage exposure. The use of these instruments can give rise to new risks and it is therefore important that the policies state clearly what instruments are permitted for use in managing currency exposure.

Most organizations, for example, if they permit the use of currency options, only allow the treasury or subsidiary to *purchase* options and not to *write* (or sell) them. Similarly, there should be controls over the use of currency borrowings to manage transaction exposures (a borrowing may be drawn down and converted into the base currency, repayment being effected by the use of a future currency receipt). Not only can this type of hedging be expensive, in terms of the margin charged by the bank, it can also create new translation exposures if the borrowing is outstanding over balance sheet reporting dates.

> *Policies should state clearly what instruments are permitted in managing currency exposure.*

In arranging hedging transactions with a bank or other financial institution an organization is creating a relationship with a new trading counterparty. As with other business relationships, all organizations should have policies to manage counterparty risk. (This is discussed in more detail in Chapter 8.) The basic features that such a policy should cover are:

Controls over counterparty risk

- the limitation of dealing to named and authorized counterparties
- the requirement for those counterparties to satisfy a stated credit rating criterion
- a monetary limit to be applied to the maximum exposure to each counterparty
- a weighting, as a percentage of the nominal value of the transaction, to be charged against the limit, and
- procedures for monitoring both compliance with the limits and changes in credit ratings.

Reporting to senior management, and in particular to the board or a subcommittee of the board, is an essential part of the control process. The policy statement should set out the basic requirements for management reporting, which should include the following:

Requirements for reporting to senior management

- the frequency of reporting
- the recipients of reports
- the content of reporting submissions, such as:
  - position reports showing hedges in place at period end and marked-to-market values
  - forecasts of net exposure and hedges outstanding
  - forecasts of future exchange rate movements
  - analysis of currency risk expressed in terms of effect of 1 per

cent movement in rates, 1 cent movement, stress testing, Value at Risk, or some other defined measure

- proposed hedging strategy for approval, and
- a statement of compliance with control procedures.

Formal approval of the policies by the board

The policies should be formally reviewed and approved by the board. This satisfies the recommendation of the Cadbury Commission in its report on the *Financial Aspects of Corporate Governance* published in December 1992 that the board should take formal responsibility for the direction and conduct of treasury management and ensures that there can be no doubt or uncertainty at board level as to the organization's treasury policies and the board's role.

Approval by the board of treasury policies is an essential element in the control framework. The other, equally important, aspect of board involvement in the control of treasury activities is the monitoring of treasury actions and compliance with policies through the receipt and review of regular and appropriately informative management reports.

Delegation of currency exposure management to a board sub-committee

The formal approval of policies and the receipt of reports by the board does not, however, prevent it from delegating responsibility for the more detailed monitoring and control of day-to-day treasury operations to a sub-committee comprising appropriately qualified personnel. If such delegation is made, the terms of reference of the sub-committee should be clearly defined and, in particular, those decisions that are reserved solely to the board must be documented.

The composition of such a sub-committee should normally include at least one non-executive director, the finance director, the treasurer, and perhaps the assistant treasurer with direct responsibility for currency exposure management. In many organizations, such a committee would also include one or more of the chief accountant, financial controller, the tax manager and company secretary.

Meetings of the sub-committee should be held on a regular and frequent basis. It would not normally be necessary to meet more frequently than at monthly intervals (except perhaps at times of unusual volatility in the foreign exchange markets), while quarterly meetings would not allow the close monitoring and rapid action that may be necessary to adjust a hedging strategy in the light of a material change in the organization's exposure to risk.

The policy statement should cover the following areas of treasury activity, most of which may have currency implications (examples of which are given below) for the organization:

This should cover the responsibilities of the board for approving policies, monitoring compliance and any delegation of responsibilities for operational oversight to a specified sub-committee, such as a Treasury Committee.

It should be noted that the Cadbury Committee's *Code of Best Practice* recommends that 'certain matters' are reserved for decision by the full board. These would include the:

- acquisition and disposal of assets of the company or its subsidiaries that are material to the company
- investments, capital projects, authority levels, *treasury policies and risk management policies* [my italics].

The Code goes on to suggest that these procedures should be set out formally in a Board Resolution, the Articles or in a Letter of Appointment.

A key aspect to be covered should be whether the treasury operates as a cost centre, profit centre or something in between these, such as a value-added service centre. The role should be defined in terms of how the treasury is to operate. The degree of centralization of responsibility for currency management in the treasury should also be defined so that the relationship between the treasury and subsidiaries is clearly set out.

This section of the manual should cover the policies in respect of the banking arrangements, balance identification and funds transmission of foreign currency receipts and payments.

This will include the management of any foreign-currency-denominated cash balances. A key policy may relate to whether these should be held in currency or swapped into the organization's domestic or base currency.

This section should deal with the funding in local currency of overseas operations and the wider issues of translation exposure management.

Interest rate risk management — This will cover interest rate risk relating to currency investments and borrowings.

Foreign exchange exposure management — This will be the section in which the foreign exchange exposure management policies will be concentrated. These policies are likely to include statements like:

Foreign exchange management objective

Foreign exchange management policies — Foreign exchange exposure management should protect the group from the adverse effects of exchange rate movements.

- The company will seek to minimize exposure by taking advantage of natural hedging opportunities.

- The company will identify and hedge exposures on a net group basis.

- Foreign exchange transactions may only be arranged in respect of actual (committed) or forecast currency exposures.

- Committed currency exposures must be hedged as soon as they are identified.

- Forecast (uncommitted) currency exposures must be hedged, partially hedged or left unhedged (depending upon the board's view of the likelihood of the exposure becoming committed and its appetite for risk). This may result in the policy setting out the maximum and minimum levels of cover that must be taken out in respect of forecast exposures within particular time periods. For example:

0–3 months	100%
4–6 months	60–75%
7–9 months	40–60%
10–12 months	0–25%

- Competitive quotes must be obtained for foreign exchange contracts in excess of £50,000 or its equivalent in foreign currency.

- Foreign exchange transactions may only be arranged with counterparties which have been authorized by the board as foreign exchange counterparties.

- Permitted foreign exchange hedging instruments include spot and forward contracts and the purchase of currency options. The treasury is not permitted to sell or 'write' currency options.

This section will cover the objectives, responsibilities and controls in respect of banking relationships for the purposes of foreign exchange management. This will include such matters as:

Banking relationships

- the criteria for selecting banks at which currency accounts will be held and foreign exchange deals transacted.

  The choice of which banks to use to carry out foreign exchange transactions should be based on the currencies in which the organization has exposures, its geographical banking requirements, the scope and quality of the services offered by individual banks and their credit ratings. Each organization should assess its own needs and select banks in a logical and structured way so that these needs can be met.

- the responsibility of the treasurer or other individual for authorizing the establishment of such relationships, and

- credit rating criteria and counterparty limits used in controlling exposure to banks.

The forecasting and reporting section will set out the policies, timing and responsibilities for:

Forecasting and reporting

- forecasting currency exposures for a stipulated time horizon by specified time periods, for example, for the next 12 months by month
- assign responsibilities for producing such forecasts
- require the forecast exposures to be netted (see Chapter 4 for a discussion of netting)
- require the treasury to produce specified actual and forecast information relating to exposures and hedges, and
- require the treasury to report on compliance with key controls.

In this section the company may set out policies relating to the processing of all transactions through the treasury computer system and to disaster prevention and recovery plans.

Treasury systems

The policy manual should be complemented by a detailed procedures manual that explains how the policies are to be implemented. The procedures manual may comprise two sections; one for use by subsidiaries and the other for use by the central treasury. Since it will contain instructions for identifying and hedging risk, as well as for the operation of the treasury control procedures, the procedures manual, like the policy

A procedures manual

manual, should be reviewed and approved by the board. A more detailed description of the contents and use of the procedures manual is provided in Chapter 8.

The organizational framework

There are, in practice, many different ways in which organizations structure the management of their foreign exchange exposure. Although the approach taken is largely determined by the size, complexity and geographical spread of the organization and its currency exposures, it is not uncommon to find organizations with very similar operating and exposure profiles taking widely differing approaches to currency management. The reasons for this divergence tend to lie in differing attitudes to risk, the relative merits of centralization compared with decentralization, and the willingness to devote resources to treasury management.

The remainder of this chapter describes the different organizational approaches, from the most simple to the most sophisticated, that are typically followed by corporate entities.

Single entity organization

In the single entity organization it is common to find that, where currency exposures arise, they are linked to a single product, or group of closely related products, sold to or purchased from one, or a very few, overseas locations. In such cases, the organization is often operating in a small niche market in which competition may be either non-existent or restricted to one or two other companies of equivalent size. It may, or may not, be possible for the company to pass on the effects of exchange rate movements to its customers through its pricing. It is not unusual to find, in such circumstances, that currency-denominated flows form a major part of the organization's revenues or costs.

As a result, the company's approach to currency management is likely to have the following characteristics:

● Where currency movements cannot be recovered through price adjustments (perhaps because fixed price contracts or catalogues have been established or because of competitive pressures), the company will be highly risk averse in its approach to currency exposure.

● It will produce detailed forecasts of currency cash flows based on regularly updated information from its sales, buying and production departments. The analysis of such currency flows typically goes down to the level of detailing individual customers, suppliers, shipments and product lines. The company will be well aware of the profit effects of exchange movements and will have contingency plans for resourcing its purchases should it be necessary.

- All sales and purchases will be fully hedged as soon as they become commitments, that is, when a firm order is placed. Cover is taken out by means of forward contracts. Depending upon the number and value of each contract, these may be arranged in any of the following ways:
  - If there are a small number of high value contracts, these are likely to be hedged individually to mature on the contracted payment date.
  - If there are a large number of low value currency receipts or payments, these are likely to be aggregated and hedged in blocks to mature in accordance with contracted settlement dates (for example, month end where payment is due 30 days after the end of the month of purchase).

- A proportion of forecast currency exposures may also be hedged where the company is both exposed to exchange risk and is confident in the accuracy of its exposure forecast. Such confidence may be based on long-standing relationships with trusted customers.

- Hedging is typically arranged with the company's clearing bank (either with the branch at which its accounts are held or a local business centre) and not quoted competitively with other banks. If a particularly significant or exotic currency is involved, the company may have a relationship with another bank solely for the purpose of dealing in this currency (and for obtaining any other facilities, such as bank accounts, letters of credit, guarantees and so on, that may be required in respect of its business in the particular overseas market).

- The company does not have a treasurer or treasury department because its currency and liquidity management requirements do not justify the expense of a full-time treasurer. Treasury functions are therefore performed by other individuals, with currency hedging being carried out by the finance director, chief accountant or financial controller.

- Currency bank accounts may be used to provide more flexibility in managing receipts and payments. Settlement of currency payments to suppliers may be made by instructing the bank to make a telegraphic transfer or by issuing a currency cheque drawn on the currency bank account. Currency receipts may initially be credited to the currency account and then debited by the bank in settlement of maturing forward contracts or, in the case of larger amounts or transactions arranged with a bank other than the company's clearing bank, the customer may be instructed to pay the currency direct to the bank's account to settle the maturing hedge.

● The policy and control framework is likely to be informal with no documented treasury policy and procedures manual, no counterparty limits, the use of the bank's standard mandate (as distinct from a specific dealing mandate) and little or no segregation of duties.

● The board receives regular reports of hedging activity.

Company with one or more subsidiaries trading overseas

Where a company has one or more subsidiaries that each generate currency exposures, there is scope for a wide variety of organizational arrangements. These are summarized below.

Subsidiaries deal directly with banks

In a fully decentralized organization each subsidiary manages its currency exposure itself and independently of other subsidiaries or the parent company. This is illustrated in Figure 3.2, in which each subsidiary deals directly with its own relationship banks. Such independence is most commonly found in cases where the subsidiaries are overseas operations in a diverse group in which there is little intercompany cross-border trade and consequently little opportunity to net intragroup currency flows.

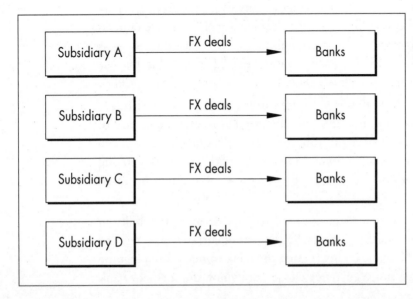

Figure 3.2

Subsidiaries deal directly with banks

Less decentralized organizations may still allow subsidiaries to manage their own exposures but may impose upon them policies and controls within which they must operate. These restrictions may include the requirement to hedge a specified level of exposures, to use particular hedging instruments and to deal with a specified list of approved banks.

The decentralized approach may be the deliberate policy of a group seeking to make local management fully responsible for the financial performance of their subsidiary or division; it may arise from a calculation of the costs and benefits of imposing a centralized group structure, not just for treasury but also for other functions; or it may simply be the result of failing to integrate acquired subsidiaries into the group culture and structure. Whatever the reason for the decentralized approach, its features and implications will often include the following elements.

- A lack of documented currency objectives and policies. Each subsidiary will develop its own policies and will feel no need to communicate them to any other part of the organization.

- The establishment of relationships with, and exposures to, local banks for the purposes of collecting, paying and hedging foreign currencies.

- Forecasting by each subsidiary, with varying degrees of accuracy, of its currency exposures.

- Hedging, or deliberately leaving unhedged, committed and forecast exposures according to the subsidiaries' internally developed policies and views on likely exchange rate movements.

- The use of potentially risky hedging instruments or techniques, which may not be appropriate for the exposures being managed or properly understood by the subsidiary.

- The absence of any reporting to the parent company of forecast exposures or of any hedging actions taken out in respect of them.

- A lack of broad professional expertise and the necessary attention as hedging is carried out by somebody performing it as a 'sideline' or fringe activity to another job. Against this, there is the likelihood that the subsidiary will be very knowledgeable about the particular currencies to which it is exposed and the banking and foreign exchange environment in its own country.

- A lack of investment in the supporting infrastructure, such as market information systems, treasury workstations, analytical and reporting systems.

The implications of the decentralized approach are that, although local management may be able to exercise greater control and take more responsibility for managing currency exposure, the group as a whole will probably suffer the following disadvantages.

- Since exposures in all the subsidiaries are not reported and consolidated, it has no overall understanding of the group exposure position and cannot evaluate currency risk.

- The absence of an understanding of the amount of its risk and its sensitivity to currency movements means that the company is handicapped in developing appropriate risk management objectives and policies.

- The ways in which subsidiaries transact hedges could increase risk rather than reduce it. Deals may be done with uncreditworthy banks or in inappropriate instruments. Hedges taken out by one subsidiary could eliminate a natural offset elsewhere in the group and increase exposure rather than reduce it.

- It is more difficult to prevent, and detect, currency speculation.

- A greater number of transactions is likely to be arranged and settled throughout the group than is necessary because opportunities to net and aggregate exposures are not available. This will increase costs in terms of administration, transfer charges and bank dealing margins.

- The application of control processes is weakened because it is more difficult to apply common standards for dealing mandates and deal documentation.

- The control of group counterparty exposure is more difficult because there is no overall co-ordination of banking relationships and limits.

Subsidiaries deal through treasury

Many companies recognize the disadvantages of full decentralization and have established central treasury functions with varying degrees of responsibility for managing currency exposure. The simplest form that this takes is that in which the treasury acts as an agent for subsidiaries in executing hedging transactions but otherwise does not play an active part in the exposure management process. This is illustrated in Figure 3.3, in which the treasury provides a deal execution service for subsidiary companies.

Where subsidiaries can deal through the treasury there may still be a large element of decentralization, either because they have discretion to use the treasury or to deal directly with banks, depending upon where they expect to obtain the most competitive rate, or because some of them are in far-off overseas locations and the difficulties of time differences and exotic currencies make it more practical for them to hedge locally. It is therefore quite common to find that, in the case of a company with a treasury in the UK, all British subsidiaries hedge through the trea-

Many companies recognize the disadvantages of full decentralization.

sury while overseas entities hedge directly with local banks. Partial centralization of this kind results, of course, in only minor benefits from improved control and more efficient dealing.

Figure 3.3
....
Subsidiaries deal through treasury

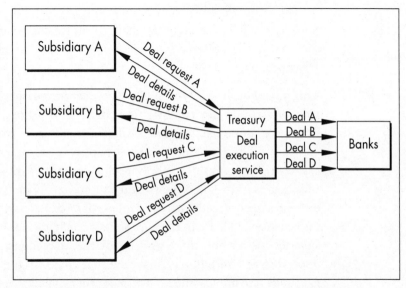

Where the treasury acts as an agent for subsidiaries, it is usual to find that it deals on demand, on the basis of a request from a subsidiary to buy or sell a specified amount of currency for a specified maturity date. The subsidiary may still have discretion whether to hedge the exposure or not. The treasury simply acts on this request by contacting one or more selected banks as soon as possible and transacting the deal at the best rate quoted to it. The deal is normally done in the name of the subsidiary and the treasury passes the rate obtained straight to the subsidiary without adding a profit margin for itself. The treasury may either confirm the transaction to the bank in the name of the subsidiary or leave the subsidiary to provide the confirmation. Settlement of the transaction at maturity is arranged by the subsidiary through its own bank accounts.

Under this type of arrangement there are some benefits to the group in that:

- There will be some information about currency exposures at the centre.
- A higher level of expertise, in terms of hedging instruments and techniques, can be applied in dealing.
- There may be opportunities for aggregating deals or for netting offsetting flows if suitable dealing requests are received from different subsidiaries at the same time.
- More effective use of banking relationships, and control of counterparty risk, may be possible.
- There is likely to be more justification for the acquisition of market information and treasury management systems to support the dealing process.

This way of dealing is typical of the cost centre treasury. It provides a service, but it does not take positions or seek to make a return for itself. There are, of course, a number of shortcomings in this approach. The company will still not have a complete picture of its committed and forecast currency exposures – only odd snapshots of those exposures that subsidiaries have asked the treasury to hedge. Again, partial hedging of exposure may actually increase rather than reduce risk. There may be no information at all about the exposures or hedging actions of foreign subsidiaries. As a result there may be a large, unrecognized and unhedged pool of exposure hidden from view that could, in the event of adverse exchange rate movements, cause major financial damage to the company.

Subsidiaries deal through a service centre treasury

A basic value-added service centre treasury will provide essentially the same service to subsidiaries but will manage the hedging with banks in a completely different way. Thus the treasury will still deal on demand from subsidiaries, but in the first instance will only arrange an intercompany transaction between itself and the subsidiary. This transaction is normally done on an 'arms-length' basis – the subsidiary receives the market exchange rate at the time of dealing and as far as it is concerned it has hedged its exposure. The treasury has now taken the subsidiary's risk onto its own book and is running an exposed position. Until it arranges external cover with a bank, the treasury (and the company) still has a currency exposure.

This approach does, of course, involve increased risks as well as providing opportunities to obtain benefits. The main risk is that the exchange rate will move adversely while the treasury is holding an exposed position, and that the currency will be eventually hedged at a worse rate than would have been obtainable at the outset. The potential benefits are that favourable currency movements will occur so that a better rate will be obtained, that an offsetting transaction will be requested, and that advantage can be taken of a natural hedge, or that the transaction can be aggregated with another exposure and a single, larger deal can be transacted at a finer rate and with savings in administration.

Clearly, this approach demands both a higher level of expertise from treasury staff and a much more rigid control environment than required in the cost centre treasury. It can be assumed that there will be strict limits on both the amounts and time periods for which exposed positions can be held, that a proper evaluation is done before it is decided to run a position, that constant monitoring of the position and exchange rate expectations is carried out, and that detailed analysis and reporting of the results of such a strategy are prepared and provided to senior management.

> *The main risk is that the exchange rate will move adversely while the treasury is holding an exposed position.*

While this approach may seem to involve taking on significantly more risk than that of the cost centre treasury, it can be argued that the risk may not actually be greater for the company, it may simply be more visible, but at the same time managed more efficiently and within a more secure control framework. However, even this arrangement imposes a major constraint on the treasury as it can still only manage those exposures for which subsidiaries have requested cover. Unreported exposures, which could make up the vast submerged mass of a currency 'iceberg' remain unidentified and unmanaged. The necessity, therefore, if the company is to avoid hidden danger, is to identify both committed and forecast exposures throughout the group, report them to the treasury and equip the treasury to manage them in accordance with the company's objectives and policies.

The treasury as group currency management centre

Where the treasury acts as a fully developed group currency management centre it will seek to manage risk and add value by taking full responsibility for the implementation of external hedging transactions in accordance with policies and strategies laid down by the board and any sub-committee with delegated authority.

In order to effect this approach the treasury requires regular, detailed and accurate currency exposure forecasts from all subsidiaries through-out the group, an ability to analyze the forecasts to derive the net group exposure, a policy framework for the hedging of the net exposure and agreed operational procedures for providing internal hedges to group companies. This arrangement therefore introduces two elements that have so far not featured in the organizational arrangements discussed above:

● a currency exposure forecast, and

● group wide currency netting of both actual and forecast exposures.

It also introduces the concept of hedging forecast exposures as well as commitments. The hedging of forecast exposures is often a subject of debate among financial managers as some would claim that it amounts to speculation in that it involves taking a position in respect of expected currency flows which may fail to materialize. The objections here are twofold: firstly to the idea of any kind of forward cover, which it is held is based on a speculative view that the rate available today is better than the rate that might be available in the future and, secondly, that the fore-cast may be completely wrong and that it is therefore foolish (and spec-ulative) to arrange foreign exchange transactions on such uncertain premises.

These objections can be countered by arguing that it is equally specu-lative to remain unhedged, particularly when there are committed receipts and payments or a price list has been issued. It would also be unrealistic to take the view that one should not hedge forecasts; if the company expects to be in business in a year's time it may well be prudent to take some action now to limit currency risk in the future. To do so would be fully consistent, philosophically, with other long-term capital investment and financing commitments that companies enter into as a matter of course. A further argument in favour of hedging forecast expo-sures is that not to do so would actually be a negation of risk manage-ment; if the company only hedges commitments out to three months, it will be fully exposed to exchange rate movements beyond the period of cover. It is likely also that, if committed exposures only are hedged, fore-casts will not be made. The company will have denied itself the ability to look far enough forward at future currency flows and exchange rate expectations to be able to identify problems early enough to take correc-tive action. The forecast enables the company to see the 'iceberg' and avoid it rather than crash into it.

As noted in Chapter 2, the currency exposure forecast should be based on expected receipts and payments denominated in a currency other than the reporting entity's base currency, and the amounts and timings of such flows should relate to reasonable assumptions about sales, production or other aspects of the organization's operations. These figures should be reported to the treasury by time period and currency (showing gross receipts and payments rather than the net for each currency) in a standard format over an agreed time horizon, such as a rolling 12-month period shown by month. Ideally, the forecast should be provided monthly to enable changing currency flow assumptions to be rapidly incorporated and covered and to allow the rolling hedging programme to proceed smoothly.

> *The forecast enables the company to see the 'iceberg' and avoid it rather than crash into it.*

The netting process, which is described in detail in Chapter 4, is carried out in order that the *true* group exposure may be identified. A mass of forecasts from group companies in a variety of locations (and therefore with a range of base currencies) and exporting to, or importing from, a range of overseas markets will present the treasury with a confused picture of group exposure in which it is difficult to determine what hedging actions are appropriate. Netting both clarifies the picture and gives clear guidance as to how the exposure can be managed.

After the forecasts have been netted the company will have identified its long or short position in each currency and each time period. Because the total value of long positions must equal the total value of short positions in each period it is easy to determine the amounts and currencies to be hedged and to hedge the agreed proportion of the exposure in accordance with the company's policies.

This hedging is carried out by the treasury and is quite separate from any internal hedging that subsidiaries may request. In effect, it enables the company to take full control over the group's net exposure position rather than allowing the hedging strategy to be determined by individual subsidiaries pursuing their particular and often conflicting objectives. The treasury's role as a group currency management centre is illustrated diagrammatically in Figure 3.4.

Clearly, one result of the netting process is that the hedging transactions arranged by the treasury externally with the banks will be quite different, in terms of amounts and currency pairs, from those arranged internally with subsidiaries. This should not create a problem when the transactions mature, as the monthly reporting process and the gradual increase in the level of cover taken should allow the treasury in the period immediately before the cover matures to have hedged only those currency flows that are fully committed and which will materialize, in both gross and net terms, at the contracted payment dates. In case of last minute problems with the receipt or payment of particular currency amounts most companies operate a system of currency bank accounts and overdraft facilities to enable them to cater for any minor timing problems that would otherwise prevent the prompt settlement of maturing foreign exchange contracts.

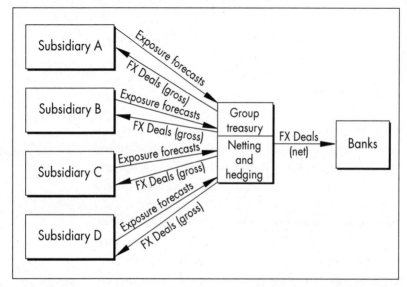

Figure 3.4

The treasury as group currency management centre

Re-invoicing centres

The re-invoicing centre is another central vehicle for managing currency exposure; it differs from the treasury centre described above, however, in that it typically does not hedge forecast currency flows and often does not deal with third party receipts and payments. The typical re-invoicing centre arranges settlement of intragroup liabilities in such a way as to relieve subsidiaries of the need to concern themselves with currency exposure.

The process normally followed is for each sale by a group company to be invoiced to the re-invoicing centre in the selling company's currency. The re-invoicing centre then invoices the ultimate customer, whether another group company or a third party, in the customer's own currency. The foreign exchange exposure is thus centralized in the re-invoicing company. Bringing exposures together in one entity in this way enables any offsetting flows to be matched and thereby minimizes the external foreign exchange transactions that are required to settle the net currency movements. Where intercompany current accounts are operated additional benefits can be obtained by leading and lagging payments and receipts.

Strictly speaking a re-invoicing centre is a currency *settlement* arrangement rather than an *exposure management* vehicle. While it eliminates the need for group companies to concern themselves with the management of currency inflows and outflows, it does not normally seek to manage currency exposure over the longer term.

The foundation for the effective, efficient and secure management of foreign exchange risk is an appropriate and clearly defined policy and organizational framework. **Summary**

The policy statement should be written and have been approved by the board. It should contain *inter alia*:

- a statement of the organization's attitude to risk and its risk management objectives
- a description of the role of the treasury
- an explanation of how currency exposures are identified and reported
- a description of how exposures are to be managed
- specific policies as to levels of cover that must be taken and the use of particular hedging instruments
- controls over counterparty risk, and
- details of management reporting requirements.

The organizational framework can vary widely from entity to entity, depending upon differences in size, complexity, geographical spread, attitude to risk and willingness to devote resources to treasury management. There are many ways to manage risk and each organization should seek to establish an approach that best suits its management philosophy and operating environment.

Part Two

4 Internal hedging

5 Foreign exchange hedging instruments

6 Hedging strategies

Internal hedging minimizes the amount of currency to buy or sell in foreign exchange transactions with banks.

Internal hedging

- Pricing
- Leading and lagging
- Netting

Internal hedging is the process by which an organization minimizes the amount of currency that it will eventually need to buy or sell in foreign exchange transactions with banks. There are three main ways in which this can be achieved:

- through pricing actions, for example by selling to overseas customers in the organization's domestic currency, or by creating receipts to off-set liabilities in the same currency
- through leading and lagging receipts and payments so that the timing of currency inflows and outflows can be matched and the flows off-set against each other, and
- by netting the remaining currency receipts and liabilities to derive the true exposure after all possible offsets have been taken into account.

Pricing decisions can reduce currency exposure considerably, but currency considerations should not override commercial needs. Maximising sales should normally take precedence over simplifying currency exposure management (although one would not, of course, price in an unconvertible currency just to secure a sale). If there is a generally accepted currency for trade in a particular industry, for example, the US Dollar for oil, or there is a dominant operator in the industry who dictates the currency of trade, it may be disadvantageous to quote in another currency as this will make it difficult for customers to compare prices or will require them to incur new currency exposures. In these circumstances, the currency of pricing will be determined by normal market practices. Where there is a choice of currency, some companies establish a policy in which authorized currencies are listed and preferred currencies, in which a discount might even be offered, identified. While the treasury should certainly advise on the currency management implications of pricing in different currencies, in the final analysis it is the need to make the sale that dictates the currency of pricing and it is then the treasury's job to manage the resulting exposure.

> *Leading and lagging and netting make it easier to identify and manage exposure.*

Leading and lagging and netting do not reduce exposure, but they do make it easier to identify and manage. While it is possible for any of the forms of treasury organization discussed in Chapter 3 to contribute to discussions about the currency implications of pricing decisions, only those treasuries that are provided with currency forecasts can take full advantage of the benefits of leading and lagging and netting. Simple timing and currency offsets may be achievable in a limited way in those trea-suries that provide a deal execution service to subsidiaries; but these opportunities are likely to be infrequent and coincidental. A fully developed treasury centre will, on the other hand, be equipped for, and indeed, have as its *raison d'être*, the management of currency exposures on a netted basis.

Pricing

We have noted above that, although exposure management should be a factor in deciding the currency of pricing for a sale or the currency of purchase, it should not take precedence over commercial needs. Commercial requirements having been satisfied, however, an organization will find that its price will probably be denominated in one of the following ways.

Where a price is in domestic currency, the management of currency exposure appears to be simplified in that, on the face of it, there is no exposure and no need to buy or sell foreign currency. While it is certainly true that there is no need to deal in foreign exchange to carry out the day-to-day running of the business, there is, however, still an exposure to foreign currency.

In its domestic currency

The domestic-currency price of goods purchased from foreign suppliers is likely to vary over time according to exchange rate movements. If the domestic currency weakens against the supplier's currency, the price is likely to rise. If a company has a number of alternative sources of supply, in different countries, this may not be a problem if it can keep prices down by 'shopping around'. If it has no alternative sources of supply, or the alternative sources are all located in the same country, it will either have to accept any increases in its domestic-currency price or attempt to hedge currency movements in the foreign exchange market. It can do this by selling its own currency forward and then, when the forward deals mature, buying it back at spot rates as illustrated in the example below. If it does operate in the currency market in this way, however, it will effectively have removed any benefit (in terms of avoiding the need to enter into foreign exchange transactions) that domestic currency pricing was intended to provide.

Example   ➤ **UK plc buys components priced in Sterling from US supplier**

At a \$/£ exchange rate of \$1.50 the supplier prices at £1 per unit to receive \$1.50 after conversion to US Dollars.

The US Dollar strengthens to \$1.40, and the supplier increases the Sterling price to £1.07 to maintain sales proceeds of \$1.50 after conversion.

The Sterling price has increased by 7 per cent as a result of exchange movements.

➤ **Hedging by UK plc**

UK plc sells £/buys \$ one month forward at a forward rate of \$1.4990.

Sterling cost = £1.00

UK plc closes out forward deal on maturity (sells \$1.4990) at spot rate of \$1.4000.

Sterling proceeds = £1.07

The gain on hedging of £0.07 offsets the price increase from the supplier.

A company selling in its domestic currency is exposed to a strengthening of its currency. This will make its goods more expensive in terms of the purchaser's currency. The purchaser is then likely to take the same action described above to obtain a cheaper source of supply.

Domestic currency pricing, therefore, while removing an overt currency exposure cannot eliminate the effects of currency movements on the business.

In its customer's or supplier's currency
....

If goods or services are priced in the customer's or supplier's currency, a clear exposure is established. In many ways this exposure can be easier to manage than the indirect exposure that results from domestic currency pricing. If prices are expressed in domestic currency terms, there is a temptation to believe that no currency exposure exists; when they are denominated in foreign currency, the exposure is clear for all to see and can be measured and managed.

Pricing in currency can be advantageous where there is another currency flow that can be matched or partially offset. For example, a British company selling to a German customer in Deutsche Marks will be happy to purchase components or raw materials priced in Deutsche Marks because it will thereby create a liability to offset its Deutsche Mark receipts. The appropriate use of currency pricing in this way can result in genuine reductions in exposure rather than purely nominal ones.

There are, however, a number of dangers inherent in foreign currency pricing. Depending upon the country involved, the treasurer may be faced with a currency that is freely tradeable, or subject to exchange controls, or simply not convertible. If the currency received from export sales is blocked, the company may never be able to repatriate the sale proceeds. If time consuming and expensive administrative procedures are required to be able to convert funds, the costs incurred should be assessed when deciding to transact business in currency.

Other factors that may influence pricing decisions are the liquidity of the foreign exchange market in a particular currency and the existence, or non-existence, of hedging instruments that can be used to manage the exposure. If it will, in practice, prove difficult to hedge the exposure, it might be advisable either not to make the sale at all or to make it only in an acceptable alternative currency.

The company should also know, when it is agreeing pricing mechanisms, whether the foreign currency is at a premium or discount to its own currency. If the foreign-currency-denominated invoice amount is determined by translating the base currency at spot rate and the base currency is at a premium, covering forward will result in a greater amount of the base currency being realized. If, however, the foreign currency is at a premium, forward cover would result in a 'loss' in base currency terms. In such a case it would be better to calculate the foreign currency price using the forward rate.

It is frequently the case that, where a company is happy to receive or make payment in either its own currency or a foreign currency, it will choose to receive a strong currency and pay in a weak currency. This is perceived to provide some advantage from exchange rate movements while, at the same time, avoiding the need to renegotiate foreign-currency-denominated prices if rates move.

It is quite common for customers and suppliers to be prepared to settle in a third currency, either because their own currency is weak or because, as above, it enables them to create an offsetting currency flow which reduces their overall exposure.

In a third currency, such as the US Dollar

Because a company may achieve particular benefits from trading in a certain currency, it may be prepared to offer more competitive prices to its commercial counterparts. These possibilities should be taken into account when a company is considering pricing decisions.

In this last case the price of a component or commodity may, for a British customer, be expressed in Sterling but this may simply be the Sterling equivalent of a foreign currency amount. For example, a French supplier prices his goods at $10 per unit. At an exchange rate of $1.50 = £1 a British customer pays £6.66 per unit. If Sterling weakens to $1.40 = £1 the supplier increases the price to £7.14 per unit.

In any of the above but explicitly related to the exchange rate for another currency

In this example, the supplier is protected against exchange rate movements. He can still receive $10 per unit for each sale if he sells his Sterling receipt forward as soon as the order from the British customer is booked. The British customer, while not having to buy Dollars is, nevertheless, fully exposed to movements in the US Dollar/Sterling exchange rate. Because the exposure is 'hidden' the customer may be unaware that he is exposed and is less able to take hedging action to protect himself. If he were to hedge the exchange risk, the customer would probably act in the way described above for hedging in cases where the goods are priced in the customer's currency.

Customers and suppliers are often prepared to settle in a third currency.

A variation on the exchange adjusted domestic currency price is sometimes found in cases where either the price is not adjusted until the exchange rate has moved an agreed amount (for example, 5 per cent versus a specified level) or both buyer and seller split the difference between them; each one bearing half the cost of an adverse movement and gaining half the benefit of a favourable change in rates.

Leading and lagging

Leading and lagging are carried out to adjust the timing of receipts and payments. 'Leading' is making a payment early, while 'lagging' is delaying payment. Leading and lagging are best suited to the intercompany settlement environment rather than for dealing with third parties. It enables a group to manage both its cash position and its currency exposures in such a way as to benefit from offsetting positions within the group.

From a currency exposure management viewpoint, leading and lagging can enable a group to adjust the timing of currency flows to eliminate unnecessary dealing or to take advantage of expected currency movements. These are illustrated in the following examples:

Subsidiary A owes Subsidiary B DEM 1 million, payable on 30 June. Subsidiary C owes Subsidiary A DEM 1 million, payable on 31 July.

Timing adjustments

Subsidiary A either obtains agreement from Subsidiary B to delay payment until 31 July or requests Subsidiary C to pay one month early, on 30 June. Alternatively, a compromise could be reached with payments being made at some point between these two dates so that B and C share the disadvantage. The result of leading and lagging is that internal sources of currency have been used and settlement has been made without the need to enter into foreign exchange contracts.

Where its base currency is weak, a company would seek to lead its foreign currency payments (pay early) and lag its foreign currency receipts. If its base currency is strong, however, it would take the opposite approach. The objective is to maximize assets in (relatively) strong currencies and to maximize liabilities in weaker currencies.

Managing exchange movements

As noted above, leading and lagging is generally only practicable *within* a group. Lagging payments to third parties, or asking customers to pay early are likely to damage relationships and can be expected to result in requests for discounts or other financial compensation (which are likely to remove the benefits obtained by leading and lagging). Equally, if the company were to lead payments or ask its customers to lag payments, it would suffer a financial penalty unless some form of compensation were forthcoming in the form of a discount or interest adjustment. This may be difficult to negotiate and to manage.

Leading and lagging is only really appropriate where there is a reasonable volume of intercompany cross-border trade and where there are no governmental or regulatory restrictions. Because leading and lagging can become complex (particularly if compensating interest payments are involved), and because it is essentially carried out to obtain a *group* benefit, there is a strong argument for a central treasury to be responsible for implementing and controlling it. Where there is a local minority interest, it may not be possible to lead and lag if local costs are incurred in order to achieve a group benefit.

> *The objective is to maximize assets in strong currencies and maximize liabilities in weaker currencies.*

Netting

The purpose of netting is to enable currency exposures to be both clearly identified and managed in the most efficient way. Efficient management, in this context, essentially means hedging exposure by means of the fewest transactions and, as far as possible, in the most marketable amounts. Netting therefore, involves the elimination of both buying and selling the same currency and the aggregation of each currency in which there is a net exposure into the largest possible amount.

The netting process discussed below relates to the method by which actual and forecast currency transaction receipts and liabilities, throughout a group and including both intercompany and third party flows, are analyzed to produce a net long or short position for each currency in a specified time period for the purposes of exposure management over an extended time horizon, usually of at least 12 months and often longer. Although a similar method of analysis applies in the case of settlement netting, the two processes should not be confused. Settlement netting is normally only used for intercompany receipts and payments and is a means of simplifying the settlement of liabilities on a spot basis.

The benefits of netting are that:

- the true group exposure can be identified and appropriate exposure management strategies formulated

- hedging in the fewest deals and the largest possible amounts should result in the minimization of administration and dealing costs and the optimization of exchange rates, and

- the risk of increasing a group's exposure, by inadvertently removing an offset through hedging one side of an already naturally hedged position, is eliminated as all hedging is carried out on a net basis.

Requirements for currency netting

The two basic requirements for implementing currency netting are a currency exposure forecast and, where currency flows are complex or large, a computerized netting system.

We discussed in Chapter 2 the basis on which currency exposure forecasts should be generated by operating companies or business units and established that the purpose of such a forecast is that it should provide an indication of the likely currency flows in each entity for future periods based on the best available information.

A suggested procedure for generating a currency forecast for submission to the group treasury is outlined below:

- The parent company should establish the level at which responsibility for developing the forecast should lie; for example, at subsidiary, business unit or operating entity level. While there may be advantages in the forecast being produced at the lowest possible level (as this is likely to be closest to the production and marketing processes), such forecasts may benefit from being reviewed by management at subsidiary or divisional level before being submitted to the treasury.

- As a general rule the treasury should seek to obtain as much detail as possible rather than allow an 'edited' version of the exposures to be submitted by the subsidiaries. The forecast should include details both of receipts and payments in the same currency and the same time period. Ideally, the forecast should be submitted monthly and show exposures by month on a rolling basis covering at least the next 12 months.

- To avoid handling a multiplicity of insignificant data, the treasury should establish a minimum level of materiality for reporting purposes. For example, amounts of less than £50 000 or equivalent in any one month need not be reported. Where the annual total of exposure is significant but monthly amounts do not reach the level at which they are deemed to be material for reporting purposes, these should be aggregated and shown, for example, on a quarterly basis.

- Clear guidelines would have to be established to deal with the treatment of exposures which may be more appropriately hedged separately from the netting process. These might, for example, include dividends from subsidiaries and capital expenditure.

- It will be necessary to identify the base currencies and transaction currencies that will be included in the netting process. A base currency is the normally the domestic currency of a company or subsidiary (although if its accounting currency is not its domestic currency the base currency will then be a foreign currency). A transaction currency is any currency in which receipts or payments are made other than the base currency.

The netting process The netting process can be performed at two levels; primary netting and secondary netting.

Primary netting Primary netting nets off purchases and sales in the same transaction currency against each base currency and thereby reduces the volume of transaction currency. An example of primary netting is shown below.

Entity	Base currency	Receive/(pay)
Subsidiary A	Sterling	USD 2 000 000.00
Subsidiary B	Sterling	USD (1 500 000.00)
Net exposure	Sterling	USD 500 000.00

In this example, our group has only two subsidiaries, A and B, both of which are Sterling based and have US Dollar exposures. Subsidiary A receives USD 2 000 000.00 from sales priced in Dollars and Subsidiary B pays USD 1 500 000.00 for Dollar priced purchases. The treasury has identified that the net Dollar exposure against Sterling is a long position (or surplus) of USD 500 000.00. In this example, the group's structure and exposures are so simple that primary netting is all that is required to identify the net position.

If we introduce more currency flows to the analysis, however, we can immediately identify the opportunities that secondary netting can offer. Let us assume that our two subsidiaries also buy and sell goods priced in other currencies and that their exposures are now as follows:

Entity	Base currency	Receive/(pay)
Subsidiary A	Sterling	USD 2 000 000.00
		DEM (5 000 000.00)
		FRF 13 000 000.00
		FRF (2 000 000.00)
Subsidiary B	Sterling	USD (1 500 000.00)
		DEM 1 000 000.00
		FRF (9 000 000.00)
		NLG 2 000 000.00
Group net position	Sterling	USD 500 000.00
		DEM (4 000 000.00)
		FRF 2 000 000.00
		NLG 2 000 000.00

If the above net group exposures were hedged on a primary netting basis, the resulting deals would be as follows:

Buy Sterling	Sell USD 500 000.00
Sell Sterling	Buy DEM 4 000 000.00
Buy Sterling	Sell FRF 2 000 000.00
Buy Sterling	Sell NLG 2 000 000.00

In this example, before primary netting takes place, the subsidiaries would transact directly with banks a total of eight foreign exchange deals, each one against Sterling, to buy or sell the required currency. After primary netting, the total number of deals required to manage the group's exposure is reduced to four. This assumes, however, that each deal will be transacted against Sterling. If all the transactions are done this way, though, the company will be buying Sterling against sales of Dollars, French Francs and Dutch Guilders and selling it against a purchase of Deutsche Marks. Clearly, it is not sensible both to buy and sell the same currency for exposures maturing within the same month or accounting period. To do so would both incur the banks' bid/offer spread and increase the number of transactions carried out and thus the administration involved in managing and accounting for them. Where there are purchases in one transaction currency and sales in another, there is an opportunity to benefit from cross-currency or 'secondary' netting.

Secondary netting allows an organization to eliminate the need to buy and sell the same currency.

In the above example, the company's computerized netting system would perform an analysis to arrive at a secondary netting solution. In essence, the calculation is quite simple and could easily be performed manually if a limited number of currencies were involved. Typically, however, there are a variety of both base and transaction currencies and a number of time periods (12 if the forecast is for the next year by month) to analyze. In such conditions, it is quicker and the risk of inaccuracy is minimized if the analysis is performed by computer.

Secondary netting with one base currency

The primary netting solution above, when secondary netted, would produce the following solution. To be able to calculate the secondary netting solution, we have to be able to translate all of the currency exposures to a common currency at the relevant spot or forward exchange rate. In

> *It is not sensible to buy and sell the same currency for exposures maturing in the same month or accounting period.*

the example below the common currency used is Sterling. The objective of secondary netting is to determine the organization's long or short position in each currency. Because each purchase of currency is matched by an equal and opposite sale of another currency the total value of the long positions must match the total value of the short positions. This is shown in the example, in which short positions are shown in brackets.

Sterling	Exchange rate	Currency requirement	Currency amount	£ equivalent
Buy	$1.5000	Sell USD	500 000.00	333 333.33
Sell	DEM 2.2900	Buy DEM	(4 000 000.00)	(1 746 724.80)
Buy	FRF 7.7500	Sell FRF	2 000 000.00	258 064.51
Buy	NLG 2.56	Sell NLG	2 000 000.00	781 250.00
			Gross currency	3 119 372.64
			Net currency	374 076.96
			Net Sterling	374 076.96

Expressed in thousands the net exposures are:

Currency and amount	Sterling equivalent
USD 500	333
DEM (4 000)	(1 746)
FRF 2 000	258
NLG 2 000	781
GBP 374	374
Total	0

The netting shows that the company needs to sell US Dollars, French Francs, Dutch Guilders and Sterling and buy Deutsche Marks. It also shows that the effect of netting has been to eliminate both buying and selling Sterling and to reduce the value of currency transactions from the gross Sterling equivalent of £3 119 372.64 to a net £1 746 724.80. The netting has therefore enabled the company to ascertain that the true exposure is approximately half of the gross exposure and indicated what deals need to be transacted to hedge the position.

The above example of secondary netting is fairly simple because it assumed that there is only one base currency (Sterling) in the group. Many international companies will, however, have operations that are located overseas and operating in a variety of base currencies. The need to net across a range of base, as well as transaction, currencies introduces another layer of complexity to the netting calculation and makes it more necessary to use a computer system to make the netting calculation.

Let us now assume that our company has established a manufacturing operation in Switzerland (Subsidiary C) that buys raw materials from, and sells its products to, other countries. The group's currency exposures now appear as follows:

Secondary netting with more than one base currency

Entity	Base currency	Receive/(pay)
Subsidiary A	Sterling	USD 2 000 000.00 DEM (5 000 000.00) FRF 13 000 000.00 FRF (2 000 000.00)
Subsidiary B	Sterling	USD (1 500 000.00) DEM 1 000 000.00 FRF (9 000 000.00) NLG 2 000 000.00
Subsidiary C	Swiss Francs	GBP 2 700 000.00 DEM 3 000 000.00 USD (4 500 000.00) FRF 8 000 000.00
Group primary netted position	Sterling	USD 500 000.00 DEM (4 000 000.00) FRF 2 000 000.00 NLG 2 000 000.00
	Swiss Francs	GBP 2 700 000.00 DEM 3 000 000.00 USD (4 500 000.00) FRF 8 000 000.00

The secondary netted position is derived by calculating the long or short position in each currency, as follows:

Sterling	Exchange rate	Currency requirement	Currency amount	£ equivalent
Buy	$1.5000	Sell USD	500 000.00	333 333.33
Sell	DEM 2.2900	Buy DEM	(4 000 000.00)	(1 746 724.80)
Buy	FRF 7.7500	Sell FRF	2 000 000.00	258 064.51
Buy	NLG 2.56	Sell NLG	2 000 000.00	781 250.00
			Gross currency	3 377 437.16
			Net currency	(116 012.50)
			Net Sterling	116 012.50

Swiss Franc	Exchange rate vs. Sterling	Currency requirement	Currency amount	£ equivalent
Buy		Sell GBP	2 700 000.00	2 700 000.00
Buy	DEM 2.2900	Sell DEM	3 000 000.00	1 310 043.60
Sell	USD 1.5000	Buy USD	(4 500 000.00)	(3 000 000.00)
Buy	FRF 7.7500	Sell FRF	8 000 000.00	1 032 258.00
			Gross currency	8 042 301.60
			Net currency	2 042 301.60
			Net Swiss Franc	(2 042 301.60)

Expressed in thousands Sterling, the group net exposures are:

Currency	UK subsidiaries	Swiss subsidiary	Group net position in Sterling	Group net position in currency
USD	333	(3 000)	(2 667)	(4 000)
DEM	(1 746)	1 310	(436)	(1 000)
FRF	258	1 032	1 290	10 000
NLG	781		781	2 000
GBP	374	2 700	3 074	3 074
SFR		(2 042)	(2 042)	(3 778)
Net	0	0	0	–

It will be clear from the above analyses that it is necessary to translate exposures into a common currency, wherever those exposures arise, in order to be able to validate that the exposures actually net to zero in each location and across the group. Once the net group exposure in the common currency has been calculated, each currency element should be translated back into an amount in the original currency, using the exchange rates that were initially used to translate them into the common currency, to determine the amount to be bought or sold.

The netting shown above indicates that the group is long in French Francs, Dutch Guilders and Sterling and short in US Dollars, Deutsche Marks and Swiss Francs. This information can be used both in the development of appropriate risk management policies (as discussed in Chapter 3) and in formulating hedging strategies. One approach that might be suggested by the net exposures in this example would be to hedge US Dollars against Sterling – which roughly match by value – and to leave the remaining exposures of the European currencies unhedged on the basis that they are, in practice, closely linked and volatility is likely to be minimal (in the short term at least).

The implications of primary and secondary netting

Clearly, it is possible to hedge exposures at either the primary or secondary levels; or at both levels if particular exposures are held back from secondary netting and hedged on a primary basis. The choice of the level of netting used can have significant implications in terms of both transaction and resource costs.

The main advantage of primary netting over secondary netting is that it is more closely related to the actual trading flows of the business and can therefore be more easily explained in terms of business need. It may also be easier to measure the profit effects of the hedging strategy as closer comparisons can be made between internal transactions (between a subsidiary and the treasury) and the matching hedge between the treasury and a bank. If external hedging is carried out on the basis of secondary netting, it is not possible to relate external deals directly to internal transactions. The two sets of deals would have to be treated as separate portfolios for reporting and analysis purposes.

The main disadvantages of using primary netting as the basis for hedging are that it may actually increase exposure, for example by removing a natural offset against another base currency, and that it is likely to be more expensive than hedging on the basis of secondary netting. Secondary netting should result in:

- a reduction in the number of transactions required to hedge currency exposures. This saves time and expense both within the treasury in

> *Without the accurate understanding of its exposures, a company will not be able to formulate and implement appropriate and effective exposure management strategies.*

dealing, confirming, settling and reporting on transactions and in other parts of the organization such as the accounting function, and

● more efficient dealing. Secondary netting typically results in fewer and larger transactions. Two-way transactions are eliminated and the banks' bid/offer margin is eliminated.

In cases where there are a range of exposures and a variety of base currencies, secondary netting is the only effective method of identifying the true exposure of the organization. Without the accurate understanding of its exposures, a company will not be able to formulate and implement appropriate and effective exposure management strategies.

Summary Internal hedging is the process by which an organization can minimize the amount of currency that it needs to hedge externally with banks. It can do this through:

● pricing actions – selling overseas in its own currency or creating offsetting currency flows

● leading and lagging of receipts and payments to create offsetting currency flows, and

● netting off the remaining currency receipts and payments to derive the true exposure for hedging purposes.

A netting analysis reveals the true nature of a group's currency exposures and provides the essential information for the development of an effective hedging strategy.

Foreign exchange instruments fall into three broad groups. In addition to these, a few companies use futures.

5

Foreign exchange hedging instruments

- Foreign exchange contracts
- Currency options
- Option-based derivative contracts
- Foreign exchange futures

Foreign exchange instruments fall into three broad groups. The first group, foreign exchange contracts, is the means by which a commitment is made to convert one currency into another currency at an agreed rate and on a specified value date. These instruments – spot and forward foreign exchange contracts – are often described as first generation foreign exchange products. The second, currency options (referred to as second generation foreign exchange products), confers on the purchaser the right, but not the obligation, to convert from one currency to another at an agreed rate. Third generation products, which can broadly be described as option-based contracts, feature characteristics of the previous two generations. They combine some of the benefits of foreign exchange contracts (no up-front premium cost, for example) with some of the benefits of currency options (such as the ability to benefit to a limited degree from exchange rate movements). In addition to these instruments, it is possible to use foreign exchange futures contracts to manage currency exposure. At present, only a very small percentage (fewer than 5 per cent) of companies use futures and these tend to be very large multinational concerns with sophisticated treasuries. Foreign exchange futures are discussed briefly at the end of this chapter.

The essential difference between a foreign exchange contract and a currency option is that the contract is a binding commitment whereas the holder of an option can choose whether to exercise it or not. The holder of an option-based contract may, however, depending upon the terms of the contract, be obliged to buy or sell currency if market rates move to a specified level during the life of the contract. This uncertainty about whether a commitment to settle the contract will arise is a key element in differentiating option-based contracts from both foreign exchange contracts and 'plain vanilla' currency options.

In this chapter we will look at the main types of foreign exchange contract, options and option-based contracts available in the market and examine the characteristics of each type of instrument.

Foreign exchange contracts

A foreign exchange contract is a *binding agreement* between two parties to exchange a specified amount of one currency for a specified amount of another currency on a particular value date or within a specified time period. Since, in every foreign exchange contract, the amount of currency to be either bought or sold is known before the transaction is arranged, the amount of the other currency will be determined by the exchange rate.

Every foreign exchange contract therefore comprises four elements:

- the currency amount bought
- the currency amount sold
- the exchange rate, and
- the maturity date.

As noted above, a foreign exchange contract is a binding agreement; once it has been entered into both sides are locked into the agreed exchange rate and it must be settled when it matures. This can be irksome when the exchange rate for the currency that has been bought or sold moves favourably after

> *A foreign exchange contract is a binding agreement.*

a contract has been arranged and, in hindsight, it would have been better not to have hedged or to have hedged at a later date. Such movements do, however, underline the importance of understanding why, and how, the market might move, of timing when to enter into a deal and of learning to live with a foreign exchange contract once you have committed to it. (They also, incidentally, prompt corporate treasurers to consider whether a currency option would have been a more appropriate hedging instrument.)

There are four kinds of foreign exchange contract. These are:

The spot contract

The simplest and most commonly used foreign exchange instrument is the spot contract. Spot contracts mature two working days ahead. For example, if on a Monday one bought Sterling at spot against the Deutsche Mark, settlement would take place on Wednesday. The two-day interval allows time for settlement instructions to be exchanged and put into effect and, where exchange controls are in force, for any administration to be completed.

Market holidays can, however, complicate the calculation of the spot value date. If there is a market holiday on the spot value date in either of the two countries concerned in a transaction, it will not be possible to settle (and therefore, to arrange) the contract. Furthermore, because most transactions are dealt by the banks through the US Dollar, it is not normal practice to settle a foreign exchange transaction if the date falls on a New York holiday. To cater for the effects of holidays, therefore, the foreign exchange market has developed the following rules for determining the spot dealing date.

- For a currency dealt against the US Dollar, the spot value date is two working days after the dealing date in the country of the currency, so long as that day is also a business day in New York. If that day is a New York holiday, the spot date is the next following business day in both markets.

  For example, for a US Dollar/Sterling transaction arranged on a Monday, the spot value date would be Wednesday. If Wednesday were a New York holiday, the value date would then be Thursday (assuming that both markets are open on that day).

- The spot date for currencies other than the Dollar against Sterling is the second working day forward in London, provided that that day is also a working day in both the country of the currency and New York.

- For far eastern currencies and the Canadian Dollar against the US Dollar, the spot dealing date is one day, rather than two days, forward. Adjustments, as described above, are made to take account of market holidays.

As a result of these adjustments, and the intervention of weekends, the spot value date can sometimes be as much as a week after the dealing date. Figure 5.1 illustrates how spot value dates are calculated where two-day settlement applies.

It is possible to deal for settlement earlier than the spot value date in some currencies. For example, one can trade US Dollars for Sterling for same day value or for the next business day. This is due both to the fact that the New York market is open after London closes, thereby allowing extra time for settlement, and to the size and efficiency of those particular markets. If, however, a currency is traded for value earlier than spot, the exchange rate must be adjusted to reflect the earlier settlement date. The principle behind this adjustment is explained later in this chapter when we discuss the calculation of forward exchange rates.

When we look at exchange rates displayed on market information systems, such as Reuters, we note that they are normally shown against the US Dollar and (with notable exceptions like Sterling) in terms of currency units per Dollar.

Foreign exchange dealers talk of direct and indirect rates, and this can cause confusion among their customers. A *direct* rate is a fixed amount

Figure 5.1

Spot value dates for two-day settlement

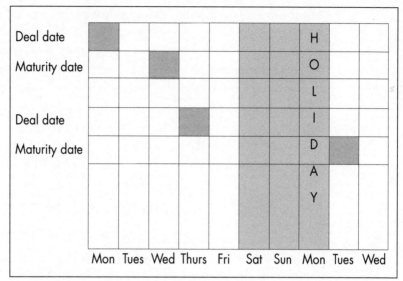

of a foreign currency quoted in terms of one's domestic currency. For example, if you are German, a direct rate against the French Franc would be expressed as follows:

$$FRF\ 100 = DEM\ 29.5630$$

An *indirect* rate is the reciprocal of the direct rate. In other words, it expresses a variable amount of a foreign currency in terms of a fixed amount of one's domestic currency, as shown below:

$$DEM\ 100 = FRF\ 338.26$$

If, however, you were a French dealer, the direct and indirect rates would be reversed. To avoid confusion between dealers located in different countries therefore, the market has standardized on quoting a variable amount of currency against one unit of the US Dollar (with the major exceptions of Sterling and some Commonwealth currencies which are quoted as Dollars per unit).

We, therefore, might see the spot rate for the Deutsche Mark quoted as follows:

$$USD/DEM\ 1.5360/66$$

This means that anyone trading Dollars can expect to buy 1.5360 Deutsche Marks for each Dollar and will have to pay 1.5366 Deutsche Marks to buy a Dollar. The difference of 0.0006 DEM (or 6 'points') between the buying and selling rates represents the bank's profit margin on the deal. This margin is also known as the 'spread' or 'bid/offer margin'. In market slang, the above rate may be referred in a shorthand way as '60/66 on a big figure of 3'. The assumption behind this is that everyone in the market knows that the DEM is trading at over 1.5 to the Dollar and that the important element in the rate is made up of the last three digits. If the rate were to move to, say 1.5295 or 1.5400, the market would then say that the 'big figure' had changed.

If we were trading the US Dollar against Sterling (a currency pair known as the 'Cable' by the market) we might expect to see spot rates like:

USD/GBP 1.5414/20

At first sight these rates look very similar to the USD/DEM rates above, the essential difference however is that this time the market is quoting the number of Dollars per Pound Sterling. We can therefore buy 1.5414 Dollars for a Pound and will have to pay 1.5420 Dollars to buy a Pound.

This difference in the way in which the currencies are quoted can lead to confusion and errors unless great care is taken when dealing is carried out. It can also lead to the risk of mistakes in calculating cross rates, as illustrated below in the examples of the French Franc/Deutsche Mark and the French Franc/Sterling cross rates. It is necessary to understand how to calculate cross rates because an important preliminary to dealing is a reasonably accurate assessment of the rate that you expect to be quoted by the bank. When you wish to deal in currency pairs that are not displayed on your market information system, you will have to calculate the cross rate yourself to arrive at an estimated rate.

Cross rates are calculated by taking the rates for each currency against the US Dollar and either multiplying or dividing them, as appropriate. Knowing which rates to take and whether to divide or multiply the answers is, of course, crucial to arriving at the correct cross rate.

Assumptions – current spot rates:

USD/DEM 1.5360–1.5366
USD/FRF 5.1977–5.1997

To calculate the cross rate to buy French Francs against Deutsche Marks,
we take the following rates:

| Sell DEM buy USD | 1.5366 | (right-hand side) |
| Buy FRF sell USD | 5.1977 | (left-hand side) |

In doing this we have both bought and sold Dollars – thereby
eliminating the USD element of the calculation – to leave us with:

| Sell DEM | 1.5366 |
| Buy FRF | 5.1977 |

$$\frac{5.1977}{1.5366} = 3.3826$$

The rate for buying FRF against DEM is therefore FRF 3.3826 = DEM 1.

In calculating the FRF/DEM cross rate (where we were buying the FRF),
it will be seen that we took the right-hand side of the Deutsche Mark rate
against the Dollar and the left-hand side of the French Franc rate and
divided the larger (French Franc) rate by the smaller (Deutsche Mark)
rate. We were able to do this because both currencies are quoted in terms
of units of currency per Dollar.

Where one of the currencies is expressed in terms of Dollars per unit
of currency (as in the case of Sterling) we have to be careful to take the
correct side of the exchange rate and to multiply rather than divide the
rates. This can be seen in the example below which shows how the cross
rate for a purchase of French Francs against Sterling is calculated.

Example Calculation of FRF/GBP cross rate

To calculate the cross rate to buy French Francs against Sterling we take the following rates:

Sell GBP buy USD	1.5414	(left-hand side)
Buy FRF sell USD	5.1977	(left-hand side)

In doing this we have both bought and sold Dollars – thereby eliminating the Dollars from the calculation – to leave us with:

Sell GBP	1.5414
Buy FRF	5.1977

$$1.5414 \times 5.1977 = 8.0117$$

The rate for buying FRF against GBP is therefore FRF 8.0117 = GBP 1.

If we were calculating the cross rate for a *sale* of French Francs against Sterling, we would, of course, have to take the rates on the other, right hand, side of the spot spread to arrive at the correct exchange rate.

Spot contracts, while being widely used, are essentially short-term instruments for those needing to buy or sell currency for immediate delivery. As such, they cannot be considered to be effective hedging instruments because hedging implies taking action to protect against adverse exchange rate movements over a longer time period. The spot contract's role as a hedging instrument, tends therefore, to be limited to actions to manage translation exposures or to the creation of currency positions to hedge expected transaction currency flows. The main instrument used to provide cover against future exchange rate movements that might affect actual and forecast currency exposures is the forward contract.

> *Spot contracts are short-term instruments for those needing to buy or sell currency for immediate delivery.*

The forward contract

A foreign exchange contract that matures on a date later than the spot value date is known as a forward contract. The main use of forward contracts is to hedge actual and forecast currency exposures that will crystallize at a future date. Through the use of a forward contract, therefore, a company can fix the exchange rate today for the conversion of a future currency receipt or payment. Forward contracts can be arranged to mature up to ten years ahead. Most contracts, however, are for maturities up to 12 months. As with a spot transaction, once the contract has been entered into it must be settled at maturity.

The need to fix the rate in advance at which currency is bought or sold arises, in practice, from the volatility experienced over the passage of time by those who have currency exposures. This volatility can be illustrated by looking at the way in which spot rates for major currencies have moved over recent years.

> *The main use of forward contracts is to hedge actual and forecast currency exposures that will crystallize at a future date.*

GBP rates at year end

	USD	DEM	JPY
1982	1.61	3.84	379.41
1983	1.45	3.95	336.83
1984	1.16	3.64	290.40
1985	1.44	3.56	289.62
1986	1.47	2.86	234.59
1987	1.87	2.96	231.13
1988	1.81	3.22	227.73
1989	1.61	2.73	231.86
1990	1.93	2.88	261.80
1991	1.87	2.84	233.70
1992	1.51	2.45	189.00
1993	1.48	2.57	165.13
1994	1.56	2.42	156.09
1995	1.55	2.22	160.16

These rates show that, from year to year, there has been great volatility in the level of Sterling; the US Dollar in particular has shown dramatic swings from a rate of $1.16 at the end of 1984 to $1.93 at the end of 1990 and back to $1.55 at the end of 1995. While, overall, Sterling has weakened steadily against the Deutsche Mark and the Yen, there have been years in which it has reversed the trend and strengthened. The uncertainty as to which way rates will move makes it difficult for corporate treasurers to manage currency positions and encourages them to take a risk averse approach by using forward contracts to close out their exposure.

Any manufacturer that imports components priced in foreign currency will be well aware of the effect that exchange rates can have on profit margins and will aim to protect against a weakening of his base currency. As an example of the impact of exchange rates on base currency costs, one needs only to look at the cost in Sterling terms of buying $20 million at the above year end rates for a few selected years. While it is, of course, unlikely that a company would buy all of its currency requirements in one go and at the year end, the rates do serve to illustrate the effect that currency movements can have and the need to manage such exposure.

Cost of $20 million at year end rates

	Rate	£ cost (000)	(Increase) Decrease (000)
1982	1.61	12 422	
1983	1.45	13 793	(1 371)
1984	1.16	17 241	(3 448)
1985	1.44	13 889	3 352
1988	1.81	11 050	
1989	1.61	12 422	(1 372)
1990	1.93	10 363	2 059

The main use of forward contracts by corporate treasuries is to hedge actual and forecast exposures so that a profit margin or a selling price can be protected. Profit centre treasuries and speculators might also use forward contracts to create long or short positions in the market in the expectation that these positions can be closed out during the life of the contract or at the final maturity date at a favourable rate and that a profit can be made.

While, in theory, the forward price for a currency can be equal to the spot price, in practice it is almost always either higher (at a premium) or lower (at a discount) than the spot price. The premium or discount represents the interest rate differential between the two currencies involved in a forward contract. If there is no difference between the interest rates for the period to which the contract relates, there will be no difference between the spot and forward prices. If, however, there is a difference in the interest rates this will be reflected in the forward premium or discount.

The forward rate is calculated by taking the spot rate and adjusting it by the 'forward points' for the relevant period. This is illustrated by the following example:

Spot and forward points might be displayed on an electronic market information system as shown below.

Spot	1.5360	1.5366
1 month	26	25
2 months	57	56
3 months	83	82
6 months	180	174
9 months	276	274
12 months	376	366

To calculate the 'outright' forward rate take the spot rate and the forward points for the relevant period, for example:

➤ **Rate to buy DEM/sell USD 1 month forward:**

Spot rate	1.5360
Forward points	(26)
Forward rate	1.5334

➤ **Rate to sell DEM/buy USD 6 months forward:**

Spot rate	1.5366
Forward points	(174)
Forward rate	1.5192

It will be noted, from the above example, that the Deutsche Mark is at a premium to the Dollar; the further forward one goes the fewer DEM one receives for a Dollar or, conversely, the fewer DEM one has to pay to buy a Dollar. Two questions arise; why is this so, and how can I tell that simply by looking at the spot rates and forward points?

The reason that the DEM in the example is at a premium to the Dollar is that DEM interest rates are lower than Dollar rates; the premium is, in effect, compensation for holding DEM rather than swapping into the Dollar to earn a higher interest rate. This is illustrated in the following example in which a holder of DEM has the choice of remaining in DEM and investing at the DEM 3-month interest rate or swapping into USD, investing at the USD 3-month interest rate and hedging the principal and interest back into DEM to eliminate the exchange risk. If the reconversion to DEM is arranged at the outset by means of a forward contract, the result is to eliminate the benefit obtained from the higher USD interest rate.

<table>
<tr><td rowspan="7">Example Calculation of three months' forward rate to buy USD/sell DEM</td><td></td><td>Interest rate</td><td>Days</td><td>Interest amount</td><td>Amount at maturity</td></tr>
<tr><td>DEM 1 000 000.00</td><td>3.1875%</td><td>90/360</td><td>7 968.75</td><td>1 007 968.75</td></tr>
<tr><td>Spot rate 1.5366</td><td></td><td></td><td></td><td></td></tr>
<tr><td>USD 650 787.45</td><td>5.375%</td><td>90/360</td><td>8 744.96</td><td>659 532.41</td></tr>
<tr><td>Forward rate</td><td></td><td></td><td></td><td>1.5283</td></tr>
<tr><td>Forward points</td><td></td><td></td><td></td><td>83</td></tr>
</table>

In the example, the DEM interest rate is more than 2 per cent lower than the USD rate. To compensate for this, the DEM is at a premium to the Dollar, with the result that, when the USD investment is converted back into DEM by means of a forward contract, fewer DEM (1.5283) are received for each Dollar than at spot (1.5366). The forward rate of 1.5283 is obtained by dividing the DEM proceeds at maturity by the USD proceeds. The 83 forward points are calculated by subtracting the forward rate from the spot rate.

The forward price for a currency is expressed, therefore, in terms of its equivalent value including interest to other currencies at a future date. The market works in such a way as to ensure that it is not normally possible to benefit from switching from one currency to another, investing in the second currency and simultaneously hedging forward the conversion of principal and interest back into the original currency. When such an opportunity arises, however briefly, the actions of arbitrageurs in taking advantage of it have the effect of moving the interest and exchange rates so that the potential for profit is quickly eliminated. Occasionally, a situation will arise in which a cheap source of funds becomes available to a particular group of borrowers, for example if a government is trying to encourage exporters by offering cheap financing of receivables. In such circumstances it is likely that an arbitrage profit could be earned on a fully hedged basis; but such opportunities are only possible when one or more elements of the normal market conditions is deliberately out of line.

It may, of course, be possible to switch to a currency paying a higher interest rate and convert principal and interest back into the original currency at the spot rate prevailing at maturity and make a profit, but this involves being exposed for the period of the investment and therefore taking a risk on exchange rate movements.

How can one tell whether a currency is at a premium or discount simply by looking at the forward points? The buying price, whether it is the spot or forward rate, must always be lower than the selling price and, for forward rates, the bank requires to make a larger margin than for spot rates. This is achieved by having a larger figure on the currency buying side than on the selling side ('falling points') when the Dollar is at a discount and the other way round ('rising points') when it is at a premium. This is shown in the examples below.

USD/DEM spot rate	1.5360	1.5366	**Examples of**
1 month USD discount	(26)	(25)	**a forward**
Forward rate	1.5334	1.5341	**premium and**
			discount
USD/SEK	6.7135	6.7235	
1 month USD premiuim	150	170	
Forward rate	6.7285	6.7405	

Two further points need to be made about forward foreign exchange rates:

- Calculations are normally made on the basis of the actual number of days elapsed over a 360-day year (except for a handful of currencies, the main one of which is Sterling, which use a 365-day year).

- For every dealing day there is a recognized one-month, two-month, and so on, value date. These are known as 'straight dates'. For example, when the spot value date is the last dealing day of the current month, the one-month straight date will be the last business day of the following month. A transaction that does not mature on a straight date, for example, one that matures in 2 months and 12 days' time, is described as being for a 'broken' date. The forward points shown on market information systems and published in newspapers like the *Financial Times* are always quoted for straight dates. As a general rule, because the interbank market tends to deal in straight dates, and it is therefore easier for a bank to cover its

> *The forward value date is the spot date plus the relevant fixed period.*

position if an exposure matures on a straight date, a finer rate should be obtainable if a corporate hedges to a straight, rather than a broken, date.

As with spot contracts, there are rules for the determination of the forward maturity date. The forward value date is the spot date (as determined in the way described earlier) plus the relevant fixed period, for example, 3 months. If this calculation results in a date on which one or both of the dealing centres is closed because it falls on a weekend or market holiday, the value date is normally the next following business day on which they are both open, but there are exceptions to this rule. These are discussed below.

The End–End Rule If the spot date is the last possible spot date in the month, the 'straight' date for fixed periods forward is also the last business day of the month in both dealing centres.

Months Rule If holidays were to cause the forward value date to go over a month end (because, for example, the spot date falls in the following month), the forward value date is fixed as the last day of the month when both centres are open. For example, a one month forward transaction is arranged at the end of March. Because of market holidays for Easter, the spot date falls at the beginning of April. The one month forward date is set for the last working day in April so that it does not extend into May.

These rules can often mean that the forward value date can be the same date on several successive dealing dates. In such a case, the rates quoted by the banks for the forward value date will, of course, differ from day to day both because the period to maturity is reducing and the spot rate is likely to be moving.

The swap contract The example on page 98, by which we demonstrated how forward points are calculated, is an example of a swap contract. A swap involves the simultaneous purchase and sale of a currency for two different value dates. In the example, the value dates were spot and three months forward but a swap could equally well be composed of two forward transactions. Where this happens, the market refers to the two halves of the swap as maturing on the 'near date' and the 'far date' to distinguish between the two forward contracts.

There are two main reasons for a corporate treasury to use a swap contract:

- to switch from one currency to another and cover the reconversion into the original currency. This is usually done to obtain cheaper funding or a better return than would otherwise be available and can be described as arbitrage in that it exploits inequalities between markets, and
- to roll over an existing contract to a later maturity date.

A British company has borrowing facilities in both Sterling and US Dollars. From time to time it is able to borrow more cheaply by issuing Dollar bankers' acceptances in New York, swapping the proceeds into Sterling and hedging the liability forward to its maturity date than by discounting Sterling acceptances for the same period.

Example of using a swap for arbitrage purposes

The company can discount Sterling acceptances for three months at an all-in rate (including bank commission of 0.25 per cent per annum) of 6.1875 per cent. On a discounted base this represents a true Sterling funding cost of 6.2834 per cent. The company aims to beat this rate by borrowing in US Dollars.

Discount $10 million bankers' acceptances at an all-in rate of 5.625% for 90 days.

Arbitrage swap

Interest $10 000 000.00 $\times \dfrac{5.625}{100} \times \dfrac{90}{360}$= $140 625.00

Proceeds $10 000 000.00 – $140 625.00 = $9 859 375.00

Proceeds sold for Sterling at spot rate of $1.5420 = £6 393 887.80

3 months' forward rate = $1.5420 less 12 points forward premium = $1.5408

Repayment of $10 million covered forward at rate of $1.5408 = £6 490 134.90

Cost of funds = £6 490 134.90 – £6 393 887.80 = £96 247.10

Effective interest rate = 6.1048%

Saving vs Sterling borrowing = 0.1786%

Interest saving = £2 815.41

An important point to note with regard to the foreign exchange swap is that the forward points for buying the Dollars for the three month forward date are taken off the spot price for *selling* Dollars rather than, as would be usual, the spot price for *buying* Dollars. In any swap deal, the customer is both buying and selling the same currency (one side being at the near date and the other being at the far date) and in normal circumstances, for example, if the transactions were arranged as two separate deals, could expect to incur the bank's bid/offer spread. Because the two transactions are included in the one swap deal, however, it is possible to eliminate the spread. This means, of course, that the customer obtains a better rate and a cheaper cost on the transaction. The effect of this in the example above is:

USD/GBP exchange rates

	Buy	Sell
Spot rates	1.5414	– 1.5420
Forward points	12	20
Forward rates	1.5402	1.5400

3 months' forward rate to buy Dollars should be $1.5402

Price of $10 million at $1.5402 = £6 492 663.20

Customer bought at $1.5420 – 0.0012 = $1.5408

Price of $10 million at $1.5408 = £6 490 134.90

Saving = £2 528.30

The other main reason for companies to use foreign exchange swap contracts is to roll over maturing forward deals. (This is often described by banks as a transaction to compensate and extend, or 'comp and extend'.) This usually occurs when a hedge has been taken out because a currency receipt or payment has been expected on a particular date and there has been a subsequent postponement, with a consequent need to extend the maturity on the original contract. Occasionally, however, a currency flow may take place earlier than the date to which it has been hedged and it will therefore need to be brought forward. A currency swap can equally well be used to do this. The important point relating to all subsequent adjustments to the maturity date of an existing hedge is that the net effect of these adjustments is to reflect only the interest rate differential between the two currencies involved for the time period of the timing adjustment. The spot rate was fixed in the initial transaction and so long as the adjustments are transacted as swaps the customer will retain the benefit (or otherwise) of the original spot rate until the deal finally matures. The following examples illustrate how swaps are used to adjust the maturity date of a hedge transaction.

> *Occasionally a currency flow may take place earlier than the date to which it has been hedged.*

A British company purchases some machinery priced in US Dollars in April. It expects to make a payment of $5 million to the supplier when the goods are delivered in three months' time at the end of July. It enters into a three month forward contract to buy Dollars against Sterling for value 31 July at a rate of $1.5402.

Extending the maturity date of an existing hedge

In late June the supplier advises the company that delivery of the machinery will be delayed by two months to the end of September. As a result, the company decides to roll over the contract to 30 September. It enters into a swap transaction to close out the original hedge and simultaneously establish new cover for a 30 September maturity date.

	31 July	*30 September*
➤ **Original hedge**		
	Buy $5 000 000.00	
	Rate $1.5402	
	Sell £3 246 331.60	
➤ **Rollover**		
	Sell $5 000 000.00	Buy $5 000 000.00
	Rate $1.5365	Rate $1.5339
	Buy £3 254 149.00	Sell £3 259 664.90
Balance on close out (received by company)	£7 817.40	

Example
Rollover of existing hedge to a later date

- The company closes out the original contract with a one month forward contract at a rate of $1.5365. The Dollar has strengthened since April and this results in a balance of £7 817.40 to be received by the company.

- The strengthening of the Dollar means that the new forward rate for September of $1.5339 is worse than the original hedge rate.

- The new forward rate to buy Dollars is calculated by taking the forward points off the selling rate for Dollars used for the 31 July closeout.

- The net cost of hedging to 30 September is £3 259 664.90 minus £7 817.40 (ignoring 2 months' interest earned on the £7 817.40) = £3 251 847.50. This is equivalent to a rate of $1.5376, which was approximately the 5 months' forward rate when the original hedge was taken out in April.

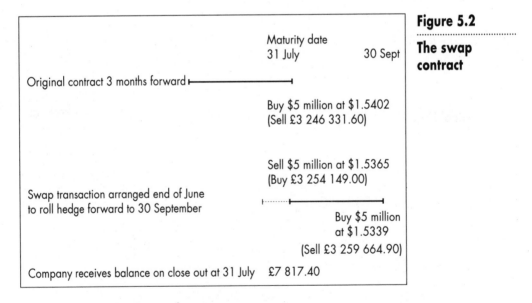

Figure 5.2

The swap contract

Maturity date
31 July   30 Sept

Original contract 3 months forward

Buy $5 million at $1.5402
(Sell £3 246 331.60)

Sell $5 million at $1.5365
(Buy £3 254 149.00)

Swap transaction arranged end of June
to roll hedge forward to 30 September

Buy $5 million
at $1.5339

(Sell £3 259 664.90)

Company receives balance on close out at 31 July   £7 817.40

In the example above the rollover comprised two forward contracts, the first for one month to close out the original hedge and the other for three months to maintain the cover of the $5 million liability. Figure 5.2 shows this example of a swap contract diagrammatically. A swap can therefore comprise two forward deals or a spot and a forward deal. Our example was straightforward, but swaps can be used to cater for a variety of more complicated situations. For example:

- The company might have wanted to extend only part of the hedge so that $3 million was payable on 31 July and $2 million on 30 September. It would therefore have only rolled over $2 million.

- It might have wanted to split the $5 million and roll some to 30 September and the balance to an even later date.

- It might have hedged too much originally and wanted to close out part of the original $5 million and roll the rest to a later date. In this case, the near date deal would be a close out of $5 million and the far date deal would be for a lesser amount, say, $4 million. When the amounts differ on each side of a swap it is known as a 'mismatched swap'.

- It may have wanted to bring forward part of the hedge and extend the balance.

There are, of course, many other combinations of actions that the company could implement to respond to a change in the timing of a receipt or payment. In the example below, the company enters into a swap to bring forward the maturity of its hedge.

Example

The company has hedged an exposure of $5 million with a three months' forward contract to the end of July. In May it is told that payment will be due at the end of June.

The company therefore enters into a swap contract to:

- buy $5 million for value 30 June
- sell $5 million for value 31 July.

This eliminates the original contract (there will probably be a Sterling balance receivable or payable on 31 July) and establishes a hedge for 30 June.

The option forward or option dated contract

The swap contract is useful for adjusting the timing of hedges in the light either of changed circumstances or simply more accurate information relating to the timing of a currency receipt or payment. Rolling over maturing contracts can, however, be administratively time consuming and, where costs are incurred in making small balancing payments to the banks, expensive. To avoid the administration and cost involved in using swaps to roll over hedges many companies use forward options (also

> *The swap contract is useful for adjusting the timing of hedges.*

known as option dated contracts) to cover the situation in which the precise timing of an exposure is uncertain but it is still necessary to hedge it.

An option forward is a forward contract that matures at two days' notice within a given time period rather than on a specific date. It therefore allows a company to cater for uncertainty in the timing of a receipt or payment and allows it to aggregate a number of currency items maturing over a period of time so that they can all be covered by one foreign exchange contract.

Thus, for example, a company expecting to pay $8 000 000 for a shipment of goods which are due to arrive in two months' time at the end of June might hedge the liability with a forward option contract if its experience is that, because of variations in the time taken at sea, the shipment period (and therefore the payment date for the goods) can vary by up to a week. Taking this into consideration, the company agrees to buy Dollars and sell Sterling for settlement on any date between 26 June and 3 July, which is the period within which it realistically expects the shipment to arrive. This is illustrated in Figure 5.3.

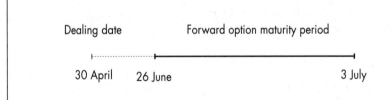

Figure 5.3

The forward option contract

Dealing date   Forward option maturity period

30 April   26 June   3 July

The company arranges a forward option contract to purchase US$8 million to mature between 26 June and 3 July. It can take delivery of the currency on any business day in this period.

Three important points need to be made about forward option contracts.

- The 'option' relates only to the date of settlement; the transaction *must* be settled as it is a foreign exchange contract, not a currency option.

- The rate for a forward option will always be the worse of the rates applying to the beginning and end of the option settlement period. This means that in the case, for example, of a purchased currency that is at a discount to the Dollar (i.e. fewer Dollars are received, or more currency is payable, the further forward one goes) the rate quoted by the bank will be that applicable to the far date of the option period. If, on the other hand, the currency is at a premium to the Dollar and more Dollars are received (or less currency is payable) the further forward one goes, the contract will be priced to the near date. This is illustrated below.

Purchase of US Dollar

➤ **Currency sold is at a discount to the Dollar, e.g. SEK:**

	Option period	
Spot	Start	End
6.7235	6.7405	6.7447

Forward option price is SEK 6.7447

➤ **Currency sold is at a premium to the Dollar, e.g. DEM:**

	Option period	
Spot	Start	End
1.5366	1.5341	1.5335

Forward option price is DEM 1.5341.

Examples of pricing of forward option contracts

● The contract can be drawn down in tranches during its maturity period. This means that it can be used to hedge a number of small amounts that would otherwise have had to be hedged individually. Not only does this minimize the administration involved in hedging exposure but it also offers the possibility, because the deal is for a large amount, of obtaining a better overall rate than would have been received for a number of smaller contracts (notwithstanding the point made above about the bank pricing the contract at the worse rate).

The company's $8 million Dollars could, for example, have been made up of 16 individual payments of $0.5 million, or eight of $1 million, or any combination of amounts and payment dates within the maturity period of the option forward. As they come up for payment it can then request the bank to deliver the funds on the appropriate date and deliver the Sterling in return. It must however, either take delivery of any remaining balance on the final maturity date or, on the last spot dealing date in the period (two business days before the final maturity date) close out or roll over any part of the contract that has not already been settled.

It will be apparent, therefore, that foreign exchange contracts provide a valuable tool for managing currency exposure. They are flexible in terms of the currencies, amounts and timing of hedges. They can be rolled over to a later maturity date, pulled forward, and closed out in full or in part. After all this, however, one element of inflexibility remains; in the final analysis a foreign exchange contract is a firm commitment that must be settled at the contracted rate. This inflexibility, in an uncertain and volatile world, has led treasurers to seek a means by which they can hedge currency exposures *without* creating at the same time a commitment to deliver, or take delivery of, currency. Such a means is provided by currency options.

Currency options

A currency option gives the buyer, on the payment of a premium, the right but not the obligation to exchange an agreed amount of one currency for an agreed amount of another currency at a specified exchange rate (the 'strike' price) on a pre-determined future date (the 'expiry' date).

A currency option therefore provides a guarantee of being able to buy or sell a currency at a particular rate without creating the obligation to do so. Because of this, the buyer of an option has a known, and fixed, worst case and at the same time the potential to benefit from any favourable movements in exchange rates. An analogy is often drawn between a currency option and an insurance policy; this analogy is particularly relevant when the cost of buying an option – the option 'premium' – is regarded as akin to the premium paid for an insurance policy.

The amount of the premium paid for an option can be influenced by the purchaser because certain of the elements that determine the price of an option are under the purchaser's control. These elements are the option's strike rate and its expiry date. The other factors that determine the price of an option are market related – the spot rate, the interest rate differential between the two currencies and the implied volatility of the exchange rate. A number of models have been produced to calculate volatility for the purpose of option pricing. The best known of these is the Black-Scholes European call option valuation formula which was originally developed (in 1973) for pricing stock options. The Black-Scholes model has since been modified by the Garman and Kohlhagen model of 1983.

There are two basic types of option – a European option which can only be exercised at maturity, and an American option which can be exercised at any time up to maturity. The buyer of an option can choose the exchange rate at which it wishes to have the right to buy or sell currency. This rate may be

> *A currency option provides a guarantee of being able to buy or sell currency at a particular rate without creating the obligation to do so.*

the same as, better than, or worse than, current market rates. Clearly, if it is better than market rates (in other words, it has *intrinsic* value) the price of the option will be higher than if it were the same as or worse than, the current market levels. If the strike rate for a European option is equal to the current outright forward rate, the option is described as an *at-the-money forward* option. If the strike rate is worse than, the current outright forward rate, the option will be termed as *out-of-the-money* and if the strike rate is better than the current outright forward rate it is known as an *in-the-money* option. Because it can be exercised at any time, the relevant market rate for determining whether an American option is in or out-of-the-money is the current spot rate. A simple method of reducing the cost of the option premium is to select a strike rate which is as far out of the money as possible. This is often possible to do when the option is being purchased to protect, for example, a budget exchange rate which is lower than current market rates.

The other factor in the price of an option which is under the control of the purchaser is the time to maturity, or 'time value'. The time value of an option is the amount by which the option premium exceeds its intrinsic value. The price of an option increases with the greater length of time to maturity. This is because, whatever the current relationship between the strike rate and market rates, one can expect rates to change over the course of time. The longer this period is the greater is the opportunity for rates to move and the greater, therefore, is the uncertainty for the bank selling the option. It is essential, when purchasing an option therefore, to identify accurately the period of exposure that needs to be hedged and to buy the option with as short a maturity period as possible if the option premium is to be minimized. It should be noted that the reduction in time value – 'time decay' – is not constant throughout the life of an option but increases (except in the case of deep in-the-money options) as the option nears maturity. The most rapid time decay occurs in the few weeks immediately before the option matures.

Both intrinsic value and time value contribute therefore, to the cost of an option; they also make up part of the value of an option during its life. Intrinsic value will alter from day to day as market rates change and time value will decay as the remaining life of an option reduces. It is possible to hold an option which has no intrinsic value (because the strike rate is worse than current market rates) but does have time value (because it matures well into the future) which is sufficient to give the option, as a whole, a positive market value. The holder of an option should always consider, therefore, whether despite having no intrinsic value the option has an overall value by virtue of the time left to final maturity. There is, in any case, always the possibility that exchange rate movements during the remaining life of the option will bring it back into the money and give it intrinsic, as well as time, value. It should, of course, not be forgotten that when an option has no intrinsic value this means that the holder of the option can buy or sell currency in the market at a better rate than that guaranteed by the option.

The use of currency options

Currency options have two main uses; as hedging and as trading instruments. As hedging instruments they are used to reduce exposure to loss while retaining the ability to gain from favourable rate movements. They also allow the user to limit the cost of hedging to a pre-determined amount in circumstances where, as in the case of a tender, a hedge may not in the event be required.

As trading instruments they are outside the scope of this book, because in this role they are used speculatively to make profits by taking a view on future exchange rate movements. I will therefore confine myself to referring briefly to the most commonly used trading strategies that treasurers are likely to come across when option trading strategies are discussed. These are:

- buying and selling options
- spreads. These involve the purchase of one option and the sale of another of the same kind but with different terms, for example:
  - vertical call spread – the options have different strike rates
  - horizontal call spread – the options have different maturity dates
  - diagonal call spread – this is a combination of a vertical and a horizontal spread.
- straddles. These are transactions that involve the purchase or sale of a number of call and put options of the same type and with similar terms.

- strangles. These comprise the purchase or sale of a number of call and put options with strike prices respectively above and below that of the current price of the underlying instrument.

- conversions. These arbitrage between the difference in the prices of options and futures.

Corporate purchasers of currency options use them predominantly as hedging tools, and for two main purposes:

- for hedging contingent liabilities, where it is uncertain whether an exposure will materialize or not but advisable to hedge in case it does, and

- for hedging normal transaction exposures.

The following examples illustrate how options are used for these two purposes.

A typical example of a contingent liability is the situation in which a company tenders for a contract. A company tendering for a contract which involves the receipt or payment of foreign currencies will have to make assumptions about the exchange rate or rates at which those receipts and payments will have to be converted to ensure that the tender price will enable it to make a profit.

Hedging contingent liabilities

At the time that it submits its tender the company does not, of course, know whether it will win the contract and therefore, whether the currency flows will take place. It cannot, therefore, take the risk of entering into binding foreign exchange contracts. If, on the other hand, the company takes no action to hedge the contingent exposures it will be fully exposed to changes in exchange rates; adverse currency movements could then eliminate the profit on the contract should the company's tender be accepted. What the company needs is a method of hedging its contingent exposure that gives it the ability, but not the obligation, to deliver or receive currency at a specified rate depending upon whether the need arises. The currency option satisfies this requirement.

Corporate purchasers of currency options use them predominantly as hedging tools.

Let us assume that a British engineering company is tendering for a contract to supply machinery to an American customer. The customer wishes to pay in US Dollars, and the company (if its tender is successful) will be in the position of receiving US Dollar 10 million revenue but having Sterling costs. It needs to price its tender at a level that enables the

Dollar revenue to be converted to Sterling at a rate which will cover its costs and yield a profit. A weakening of the Dollar would reduce the Sterling value of the sales revenue, reducing the profit and possibly eliminating it altogether. A strengthening of the Dollar, on the other hand, would increase the Sterling proceeds. The company needs therefore, to hedge against a weakening of the Dollar and has calculated that it needs to convert its Dollars at a rate of $1.6000 = £1 in order to make its required profit margin on the contract.

There will be a period of one month between the submission of the tender and the announcement of the winner of the contract. The company's exposure is therefore for a period of one month; when the winner is announced the company will either have no exposure (if it loses the contract) or a committed exposure (if it wins the contract). The committed exposure can then be hedged by the company using, for example, forward contracts. The company's action is illustrated in Figure 5.4.

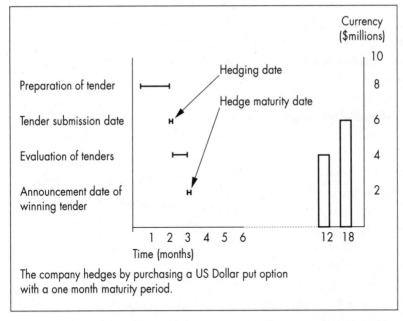

Figure 5.4

Using currency options to hedge contingent exposures

The company hedges by purchasing a US Dollar put option with a one month maturity period.

The company therefore purchases an option to sell 10 million Dollars and buy Sterling (a 'Dollar put' option) at a strike rate of $1.6000 expiring in one month. It pays a premium (expressed as a percentage of the $10 million covered) to the bank as the fee for the purchase of the option and builds the cost of the fee into its tender price. The company is now protected against the risk of a weakening of the Dollar but is not committed to sell Dollars to the bank. It is now able to cope with any potential outcome.

The possible outcomes will be that the company has either won or lost the contract, and that the Dollar will have strengthened, weakened (or stayed at the same level) against Sterling. Let us look at each of these in turn.

➤ The Dollar has strengthened to $1.5500

In this case, the company allows the option to lapse and arranges forward contracts to sell Dollars based on the current spot rate of $1.5500. As a result, it receives more Sterling than it expected and realizes a larger profit on the contract.

➤ The Dollar has weakened to $1.6500

In this case, the company exercises the contract to sell Dollars at $1.6000. It may do this by simply exercising the contract or by selling it back to the bank from which it was purchased.

At this stage, of course, the company has not received any US Dollar flows, it simply knows that such flows will definitely occur in the future. If it exercises the option to sell Dollars it must at the same time purchase the Dollars it has sold. It does this at the current spot price of $1.6500 at a Sterling cost of £6 060 606. The receipt from the option is £6 250 000 and the company has therefore realized a gain of £189 394. This gain offsets the 'loss' incurred by the company in hedging the exposures using forward contracts.

Alternatively, the company could sell the option back to the bank and receive the market value of the option. This should yield the same proceeds as exercising the option and again these are offset against the worse hedging rate that results from the weakening of the Dollar.
Ignoring the effect of the forward points (and the premium) the result of using the option has been:

		£ value of $10m
Spot rate at tender date	$1.6000	£6 250 000.00
compared with:		
Spot rate at hedging date	$1.6500	£6 060 606.00
Gain on option		£ 189 394.00
Total		£6 250 000.00

If the current spot rate is the same as the option strike rate on the option's maturity date there will be no net difference to the company in exercising the option or letting it lapse.

If the company does not win the contract, it will not, of course, need to hedge any future exposures, but it will still have the currency option which may, if it is in the money, have value. The potential outcomes might be:

Example B. The company does not win the contract

➤ **The Dollar has strengthened to $1.5500**

The option has no value and the company allows it to lapse. The net cost to the company of issuing the tender is the option premium.

➤ **The Dollar has weakened to $1.6500**

The company exercises or sells back the option and makes a profit of £189 394.00.

Hedging transaction exposures

Currency options are increasingly being used by corporate treasurers to hedge transaction exposures when a company wishes to lock into an exchange rate but at the same time be able to take advantage of any favourable movement in rates.

For example, a British company has to pay $10 million to a supplier in six months' time. The current spot rate is $1.6000 and the six months' forward rate is $1.5700. The company wants to protect itself against the risk of the Dollar strengthening to a rate better than $1.5500 (which is its budget exchange rate) but would also like to be able to benefit if the Dollar weakened over the next six months.

It therefore purchases an out-of-the-money forward option to buy $10 million (a 'Dollar call') and sell Sterling at a rate of $1.5600 with a six months' maturity. The option premium reduces the effective exchange rate on the option to $1.5500 – the company's budget rate.

Examples of the possible outcomes are illustrated below.

Example
Using options
to hedge
transaction
exposures

> ### The Dollar strengthens to $1.5000

The company exercises the option to buy Dollars at the better rate of $1.5600 and realizes an effective rate of $1.5500 after taking the cost of the premium into consideration.

> ### The Dollar strengthens to $1.5700

The company allows the option to lapse and buys Dollars at $1.5700. After taking the premium into account it has achieved an effective rate of $1.5600, which is better than the effective option rate of $1.5500 but worse than the original forward rate of $1.5700.

> ### The Dollar weakens to $1.6200

The company allows the option to lapse and buys Dollars at the market rate of $1.6200.

Advantages of using currency options

Currency options provide a number of benefits, which can be summarized as follows:

- They offer the ability to benefit from a favourable movement in exchange rates while, at the same time, providing a known 'worst case' because the downside risk is cut off at the level of the strike rate.
- They provide flexibility through the ability of buyers to select the strike rate that is most appropriate to the purpose for which they require the hedge.
- They enable buyers to hedge where the underlying transaction is uncertain. The ability to hedge contingent exposures is perhaps the greatest single benefit provided by currency options.

Disadvantages of currency options

There are a number of implications from using options that may, depending upon one's viewpoint, be considered to be disadvantages. Among these are:

- the necessity of paying a premium (although, as we will see later in this chapter, the premium can be reduced or eliminated altogether if the treasurer is willing to give up some of the benefits of an option). The size of the option premium is the biggest single disincentive to potential buyers of options.

- the difficulties encountered in valuing options during their lives, particularly at balance sheet dates

- the need to explain to senior management how they work and why they are more appropriate in any particular circumstances than other forms of hedging, and

- the need for a properly considered strategy for the exercise or sale of options to ensure that maximum benefit is derived from their use and the need for continuous monitoring to effect the strategy.

The examples set out above illustrate the uses of options to cover both contingent and committed exposures. In both cases the company has had to pay a fee (the premium) to purchase the option. As noted above, a key objection to options for most users, and potential users, is that they involve the payment of an often substantial premium for an instrument which, in the event, may not be used. To overcome this disadvantage, the foreign exchange market has developed a number of variations on currency options that provide some of the benefits of options while at the same time substantially reducing or even eliminating the premium cost. These can perhaps best be described as option-based derivatives contracts, because in eliminating the premium cost they also eliminate in whole or in part the indispensable characteristic of an option – that the holder can choose whether to exercise it or not. Many of the option-based derivative contracts involve the simultaneous purchase and sale of options and thus confer upon each counterparty the right to exercise the option against the other. The most common option-based derivatives are described below.

Option-based derivative contracts

Option-based derivatives are created by combining derivatives to create instruments with new characteristics. The most frequently used currency derivatives are described below.

Deferred premium or 'Boston' options

This option allows the purchaser to defer the payment of the premium. If the option is not exercised, the premium is payable when the option expires. If the option is exercised, the premium is included in the value for the settlement of the transaction. The cost of a deferred premium option is generally higher than that for an ordinary option in order to compensate the bank for the deferral in the payment of the premium.

This product, which was originally developed by the Bank of Boston, is often called a Boston option.

A compound option is an option on an option. It works in the following way.

A buyer of a compound option pays a premium for the first leg of the structure, which is known as the compound call. This gives the buyer the right, but not the obligation, to buy a specified ordinary option at a pre-determined price on a pre-determined future date (the second leg). If the buyer decides to take up his right to purchase the ordinary option, he will acquire the same rights as for the currency option described above – that is, either to exercise the option or let it lapse. He will, of course, only exercise his right to purchase the second leg of the option if the same option cannot be obtained more cheaply elsewhere in the market.

The cost to the buyer of the compound option is the combined premiums of the two legs. The total cost should never be greater than this because, as noted above, the buyer will only pay the premium for the second leg if the pre-agreed premium is cheaper than the current market cost of a similar option.

The main benefit of a compound option is that it enables a buyer to minimize at the outset the premium cost of cover taken in cases where it is not certain that an exposure will eventually materialize. This is illustrated in the example below.

A British company forecasts that it may have to buy Dollars in twelve months' time, but it will not be able to confirm this for three months. It is worried that in the meantime Sterling may weaken against the Dollar and seeks to hedge against this risk without creating a commitment to buy Dollars. The company has considered buying an ordinary option but does not wish to pay the premium cost.

It therefore buys a compound option in which the first leg is a three month compound call option giving the company the right to buy a nine month Sterling put/Dollar call option with a strike rate equivalent to the current twelve month forward exchange rate (at-the-money forward).

It pays an up-front premium of 1.25 per cent for the first leg of the call and agrees a premium of 3.20 per cent payable for the ordinary option if it is taken up in three months' time. The maximum cost of the compound option, if taken up, is therefore 4.45 per cent of the principal amount in Sterling terms.

In three months' time, if the company confirms that the exposure will arise, it will consider exercising its right to purchase the second leg of the option. It will only do this if the pre-agreed premium cost of 3.20 per cent for the nine month ordinary option (the second leg) is less than the cost of a similar option in the market at that time.

When the compound option was originally priced, the cost of an ordinary twelve month at-the-money forward option was 3.75 per cent. While the maximum cost of the compound option is therefore greater than that of an ordinary option for the same maturity and strike rate, it should be noted that the initial premium for the first leg was a third of the cost. If the hedge were not, in the event, needed the company has only incurred an outlay of 1.25 per cent instead of 3.75 per cent for the twelve-month option. This can be a very cheap way of hedging a contingent liability and offers the purchaser the opportunity, even if the underlying currency flow does not materialize, of exercising the second leg of the option if there is an opportunity in the market to profit by doing so.

Cylinder options Where a company has a definite exposure that it wishes to hedge but it does not wish to pay the full premium for an ordinary foreign exchange option it may find a cylinder option (also known as a range forward or zero cost option) an attractive alternative. Cylinder options can be structured so that the premium is greatly reduced or even eliminated entirely. The reason for this is that the premium payable by the company to the bank for the option that it has purchased is offset by the premium receivable by the company from the bank for the option that the company has sold to the bank. In seeking to eliminate the premium cost, the company has granted to the bank the right to buy or sell currency to it. The company should not, therefore, enter into a cylinder option unless it is certain that it has an underlying currency flow.

Cylinder options reduce or even eliminate the premium.

A typical cylinder option is illustrated below and in Figure 5.5.

A British company has exported goods to a US customer and expects to receive payment in Dollars in three months' time. The company expects the Dollar to strengthen against Sterling in this period but is not confident enough to leave the exposure unhedged and does not want to pay the full premium cost of an ordinary currency option.

The company enters into a cylinder option in which it buys an option to lock into a nominated exchange rate (strike A) for the three months and at the same time sells (or writes) an option to the bank for the same period with a different strike rate (strike B). The values of both options are equal and the premium payments between the counterparties net to zero.

Current spot rate	**$1.6000**
Three months forward points	**–0.0030**

The company buys a Sterling call/Dollar put option at $1.6200 (strike A) and sells a Sterling put/Dollar call at $1.5700 (strike B).

If, at the maturity of the option, the market spot rate is between the two strike rates both options will expire out-of-the-money. The company will then sell its Dollars in the market at the current spot rate.

If the spot rate is higher than $1.6200 the company will exercise its right to sell Dollars to the bank at strike rate A – $1.6200.

If the spot rate is below $1.5700, the bank will exercise its option to buy Dollars from the company at strike rate B – $1.5700.

The company therefore knows that, as a result of the option, it cannot get a worse rate than $1.6200 but can benefit if the Dollar strengthens to $1.5700. It cannot benefit from any further strengthening of the Dollar beyond $1.5700 because at that rate the bank will exercise its option to buy Dollars from the company.

The principal difference between the cylinder option and an ordinary option is that the cylinder option involves the writing of an option at the same time as the purchase of one. In our example this has several effects: it reduces or eliminates (depending upon the strike rates chosen) the premium; limits the upside potential for the company and creates an obligation for it to sell Dollars to the bank at strike rate B. The creation of this obligation to sell Dollars makes it essential that the company should be sure that it has an underlying currency flow. If it does not, it will have to buy Dollars in the market or buy back the bank's option. Each of these courses of action will result in a loss for the company if the bank exercises its right to buy Dollars from the company.

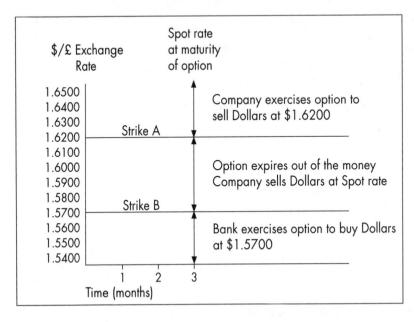

Figure 5.5

Example of a cylinder option

It should be noted that, in cases where the two strike rates of a cylinder option are close together, a cylinder may not be any more advantageous than a forward foreign exchange contract.

Cylinder options can be arranged in most major currencies and for amounts as low as $100 000.

Participating forwards

A participating forward also allows a buyer to reduce or eliminate the premium cost while at the same time guaranteeing a 'worst case' rate and the potential to benefit from favourable movements in exchange rates. The potential to gain is, however, limited to a proportion of the total exposure. An example of a participating forward is shown below.

A British company sells to a US customer in Dollars and is due to be paid in six months' time. It wishes to lock into an exchange rate while retaining the ability to benefit from any strengthening of the Dollar, but wants to avoid paying an option premium.

The company buys an option for the full value of its exposure and at the same time sells an option with the same strike rate for a proportion of the exposure. Any gain that results from favourable exchange rate movements will be shared with the bank. The company's Dollar receivable is $10 million.

The current spot rate is $1.6000 and the six months' outright forward rate is $1.5935.

The cost of the participating forward is reflected in the strike rate, which is set at $1.6300 – 3 cents out-of-the-money. The company buys a Dollar put/Sterling call for $10 million and sells to the bank a Dollar call/Sterling put at $1.6300 for $5 million.

If, on expiry, the spot rate is below $1.6300 the bank will exercise the Dollar call option for $5 million against the company, making it sell Dollars at $1.6300. The company then enters the market to sell the remaining $5 million at the current market rate.

If, on the other hand, the pound has strengthened to above $1.6300, the company will exercise its Dollar put option for the full $10 million at the strike rate of $1.6300.

In this example it will be noticed that the strike rate was set three cents out-of-the-money. In effect, the premium cost has been built into the strike rate and the Dollar therefore has to strengthen by three cents before the company starts to benefit from the hedge. At the same time, because it has sold an option to the bank, it loses part of its benefit from any strengthening of the Dollar.

Participating forwards are frequently used by companies that operate active hedging strategies and wish to hedge a worst case at minimum cost while retaining the ability to benefit from favourable rate movements. Because the participating forward involves selling an option to the bank, a company should only use this instrument when it is certain that the currency flow will take place.

Knock-out options

A knock-out option incorporates an exchange rate at which, if it is reached in the market, the option will become inoperative, or 'knocked out'. This rate is known as the knock-out level and the cost of the option is largely determined by how close the knock-out level is to the current spot rate. If the knock-out level is close to the prevailing spot rate, the option will be relatively cheap; the farther away it is from spot rate the more expensive it will be and the closer its price will be to an ordinary option. A knock-out option should, however, always be cheaper than an ordinary option.

A knock-out option enables a hedge to be put in place more cheaply than for an ordinary option, protects against downside risk and at the same time allows the buyer scope to put a new hedge in place at a better rate should the knock-out level be reached. It is important to note that as the knock-out level is operative *throughout* the life of the option, not just at maturity, a knock-out option therefore requires constant monitoring of exchange rates if market rates get close to the knock-out level at any time.

> *A knock-out option should always be cheaper than an ordinary option.*

The following example illustrates how the knock-out option works.

Example of a knock-out option

A British company has to pay US Dollars in six months' time. The company has a strong view that Sterling will not strengthen against the Dollar during this period.

The current spot rate is $1.6000 and the outright six months' forward rate is $1.5935.

The company could cover forward at $1.5935, buy an at-the-money forward option at a cost of 2.5 per cent, or a knock-out option with an at-the-money forward strike rate of $1.5935 and a knock-out level set at $1.6500 for a premium cost of 2.0 per cent. Because it does not expect Sterling to strengthen it decides to enter into a knock-out option.

If Sterling strengthens to a level above $1.6500 (the knock-out level) during the life of the option the company will lose the cover of the option. The company will, however, be able to hedge the exposure again, by a new option or an outright forward contract, at this much better rate.

If Sterling weakens against the Dollar, the company is protected at the rate of $1.5935 until the option matures *unless* the rate should at any time move back up to the knock-out level at which point the cover would be lost (but a new hedge at this favourable rate could be taken out).

Knock-out options are also known as barrier options. Another kind of barrier option is the 'knock-in' option, which becomes operative when a pre-determined rate is reached in the market and which works in a similar way to the knock-out option.

Average rate options are also known as Asian options and are often used in managing translation exposures, particularly those relating to profits earned by foreign subsidiaries. Where a company is exposed to movements in exchange rates over time it may, as an alternative to buying a 'strip' of options, wish to use an option in which the strike rate is compared with the average movement in the exchange rate. The average rate option (AVRO) answers this need. **Average rate options**

For the payment of an up-front premium, the purchaser of an AVRO is protected against adverse movements in the average exchange rate relative to the strike rate for a pre-determined period, while at the same time is able to benefit from any favourable movements in rates. A strike rate is agreed for the AVRO and this is compared with the average rate over the period, calculated by reference to an accepted marker rate such as the central bank fixing rate for the currency pair or the rate quoted by a specified bank at a specified time in a particular market (e.g. 11 am in London).

An AVRO might be used, for example, in the case of an company making monthly repayments on a foreign-currency-denominated loan over, say, 12 months. The treasurer may wish to hedge against the risk of a fall in the average value of his base currency against the foreign currency while, at the same time, retain the ability to benefit from a strengthening of his currency. The treasurer could purchase an AVRO and, to match the timing of the rates used in calculating the average rate over the period, arrange his foreign exchange transactions to buy the currency for the loan repayments as closely as possible to the time that the reference rate is recorded.

When the AVRO expires, the average of the reference rates is calculated and, if this is worse than the strike rate of the AVRO, the company is paid an amount representing the difference between the two rates (settlement taking place two days after the expiry of the AVRO). If, on the other hand, the calculated average rate is in the company's favour this suggests that it has been able to obtain a better rate than that which was protected by the AVRO and no compensation will be payable to the company. Clearly, if the company has matched its purchases closely to the rates used in calculating the average rate it will have achieved a good hedge; to the extent that it has been able to obtain better rates than those making up the average rate it will have made a 'gain' on the hedge.

The cost of an AVRO in the example above in which the strike rate is set as the six months outright forward rate, should be less than the cost of buying a strip of 12 at-the-money forward ordinary options. One reason for this is that average rate options reduce volatility. AVROs are available for most major currencies in amounts of US $100 000 per fixing date and generally for a maximum period of two years, although this can be extended to five years for certain currencies.

Lookback options

These are similar to average rate options except that, instead of using average rates, a lookback option uses the most favourable rate among all of the spot rates during its life. This feature of the lookback option maximizes their volatility and makes them more expensive than comparable ordinary options.

Tender to contract 'TTC' options

Tender to contract options are designed for companies that are involved in tendering for very large contracts which would involve the payment of significant premiums if they were fully covered by options.

The TTC option allows the buyer to pay only 10 per cent of the premium at the time of submitting its tender. The balance of the premium is payable only if the tender is successful. If the tender is unsuccessful, the option lapses automatically and cannot be used against other contracts or exercised in the market if rates have moved favourably in the meantime. TTCs can be considered expensive if one takes into account the fact that approximately three-quarters of tenders are unsuccessful.

> SCOUTs have a number of benefits for both tenderers and contract awarders.

Shared currency option, under tender ('SCOUT')

This type of option enables tenderers to share the premium cost of an option while, at the same time, giving each tenderer full cover in the event that its tender is successful. This is effected by the awarder of the contract purchasing an option and then charging the tenderers for an equal share of the premium cost. When the contract is awarded, the successful tenderer takes over the option and is thus provided with full cover of the exposure.

A foreign government invites UK contractors to tender for a project in which payment will be made in US Dollars. The expected maximum contract value is $100 million and the current spot rate against Sterling is $1.50.

The government purchases an option for $100 million at a cost of 3 per cent and agrees with the bank that it will be used as a SCOUT. Each of the five tenderers is required to contribute 0.6% as their share of the premium paid.

The successful contractor will be given all rights under the option on the day that the contract is awarded and will therefore have obtained full cover at only one-fifth of the cost.

The unsuccessful tenderers will have benefited to the extent that their loss (the premium cost incurred) will only be a fifth of that which they would have lost had they had to pay the full premium.

SCOUT contracts usually include a clause to the effect that, if a contract is not awarded or is delayed, any profit that results from the exercise of the option is shared among the group of tenderers.

SCOUTs have a number of benefits for both tenderers and contract awarders. The main advantages being that the SCOUT:

- provides the tenderer with full cover at a fraction of the normal premium cost
- allows the tenderer to bid more competitively as hedging costs are reduced, and
- enables the tenders to be more comparable as differences in hedging and currency exposures are eliminated.

Other derivatives

Other third generation foreign exchange products are described briefly below. It is not likely that the average corporate treasurer running a value-added service centre treasury will use such options so they have been included here mainly for reference purposes.

Digital (or binary) options

These options have only two possible outcomes; a zero pay-off if they expire out-of-the-money and a pre-determined value if they expire in-the-money. Digital options are generally cheaper than comparable ordinary options unless the pre-determined pay-off is set at a very high level.

Chooser (or double) options .... At origination these are not specified as either put or call options. The purchaser can choose, on a specified date, whether the option is to be a put or a call. Chooser options are more expensive than ordinary put or call options but cheaper than a combination of the two.

The pay-later option .... This is similar to an ordinary option except that no upfront premium is payable. If the option expires out-of-the-money, no premium is payable, while if it expires in-the-money, a pre-determined premium is payable; in which case the premium will be greater than that for an ordinary option.

The currency option market is both active and innovative; the contracts described above are only some of the more commonly used instruments among a wide variety of option-based hedging tools. Inevitably, the corporate treasurer will encounter other types of contract which have not been described in this chapter. An understanding of the basic principles of options, as set out above, should, however, enable the treasurer to identify rapidly the implications and benefits offered by any new type of instrument.

Exchange traded options and over the counter (OTC) options
....

Currency options are available either from a recognized exchange, in which case they are known as *exchange*, *traded*, or *listed* options or direct from banks as *'over the counter'* options.

Exchange traded options .... These are standardized options dealt on a recognized exchange. They are available only in multiples of a pre-determined standard amount and are limited to specified currencies. They also have fixed maturity dates (which on the majority of exchanges is the third Wednesday in the months of March, June, September and December) and a maximum period of 12 months. Exchange traded options also have pre-determined exercise prices which are set using formulae based on the standard maturities. Most currency options that are traded on an exchange are *American options*.

Exchange traded options are guaranteed by the exchange and, because of the risk that the exchange is thereby taking on, the option writer is required to maintain a margin with the exchange.

Because the options are standardized it is possible for the exchange to quote firm rates. The existence of these publicly quoted rates provides a foundation to the market that enables the existence of an active secondary market.

The leading exchanges on which options are traded are:

- the Philadelphia Stock Exchange
- the Chicago Mercantile Exchange
- the European Options Exchange (located in Amsterdam)
- the London International Financial Futures Exchange (LIFFE)
- the London Traded Options Market
- the Singapore International Monetary Exchange
- the New Zealand Futures Exchange.

These are sold or bought by banks and are typically tailored to the individual customer's requirements with regard to the currency, amount, maturity and strike rate. OTC options are therefore much more flexible than exchange traded options and tend to be used in preference to traded options by corporates. All of the option-based derivatives described above are over the counter products.

Over the counter options

A thriving secondary market for options is in operation, which involves the sale or resale of an option by a counterparty other than the original writer of the option. There are secondary markets in both exchange traded options (facilitated by the standardization and publicly quoted daily prices) and for OTC options that have been issued in accordance with recognized terms. In the UK, the standard for over the counter options has been established by the British Bankers Association for the London Interbank Currency Options Market (LICOM).

Trading on the secondary market is principally interbank and relates to the resale of unexpired exchange traded options issued and transacted externally to the exchange and to unexpired over the counter options that have been repurchased either by the original writer or another party.

Foreign exchange futures

Foreign exchange futures are available, in the same way as traded options, on a number of exchanges. They are sold in standard amounts for standard maturities and in a limited range of currencies. A corporate customer that wished to buy futures would normally buy them through a bank or broker that is a member of an exchange.

A currency futures contract can be used to protect against fluctuations in exchange rates. A contract can be entered into either to sell currency or to buy it. The selling of a contract (known as a 'short hedge') will result in a profit if the currency sold weakens. The buying of a futures contract (a 'long hedge'), on the other hand, will yield a profit if the currency bought strengthens.

A futures contract, unlike a currency option, is a commitment that must be settled or closed out by the time it matures.

A number of important points need to be made with regard to the use of futures.

- While each exchange is independent and determines the contracts it will trade and the rules under which it operates, there are a number of features that are common to all of the exchanges.

> *A currency futures contract can be used to protect against fluctuations in exchange rates.*

Among these are the ability to close out a contract at any time by transacting an equal and opposite contract; that all contracts are guaranteed by the clearing house that is operated by the members of the exchange; that prices are publicly quoted and that members are required to deposit cash margins in respect of all outstanding contracts on the exchange.

- Exchange members, because they are obliged to deposit a margin for each contract, call in turn for margins from their customers. The margin consists of an *initial margin*, which is a fixed amount per contract payable when the deal is arranged, and a *variation margin*, which covers any unrealized losses on outstanding contracts and is calculated daily. If unrealized profits arise, the clearing house pays money back to its members and they may pass this back to their customers if this has been contractually agreed.

- Each futures contract has three key dates. These are:
  - the delivery month
  - the delivery day. This is the day in the delivery month on which settlement is to be made.
  - the last trading day. This is the last day in the delivery month on which a particular contract can be bought or sold on the exchange.

  For each exchange, the relevant dates are fixed for each type of contract. Many exchanges use, for example, March, June, September and December as the delivery months for futures contracts.

- Futures contracts are not normally settled by delivery of the underlying currency. The majority are closed out by means of an equal and opposite transaction in the same market and a gain or loss is settled in cash. As a hedging tool, therefore, a currency futures contract is normally used to protect an exchange rate; the actual purchase or sale of currency is normally effected by a subsequent spot or forward foreign exchange transaction.

A British company orders some raw materials in September from a US supplier for delivery (and payment) in three months' time (i.e. December). The cost of the materials is $450 000. The company could simply buy the Dollars at the current forward rate of $1.50 = £1 but instead chooses to hedge using futures.

Example of a currency future

It sells 12 LIFFE £25 000 Sterling contracts for December delivery at the market rate of $1.50 = £1 (and pays its initial margin).

By December the spot rate has moved to $1.40 = £1. The effect of the hedge is as follows.

Sold rate per contract	$1.50
Bought rate per contract	$1.40
Profit in ticks (0.0001) per contract	1 000
Tick value	$2.50
Number of contracts	12
Profit (12 x 1,000 x $2.50)	$30 000
Converted to Sterling at spot of $1.40	£21 429
Cost of $450 000 at spot rate	£(321 429)
Net cost of $450 000	£300 000
Effective exchange rate	$1.50

In the next chapter we will discuss the use of foreign exchange instruments, including options, as well as other techniques in implementing hedging strategies.

Summary In this chapter I have described the different types of instrument that can be used to hedge actual, forecast and contingent foreign exchange exposures. We have seen that foreign exchange contracts create a commitment to exchange one currency for another at a specified rate and maturity date, while currency options, for the payment of a fee, enable the user to guarantee a rate while still allowing the opportunity to benefit from favourable exchange movements. Option based derivatives combine some of the features of foreign exchange contracts with those of currency options to provide another level of flexibility in the management of currency risk.

The treasurer therefore has access to a wide range of hedging instruments with which to manage an organization's foreign exchange positions and to implement its hedging strategies.

The approach to
an organization's
hedging strategy
depends on its
attitude to risk.

6

Hedging strategies

- Developing a hedging strategy
- Strategies for different kinds of treasury
- Strategies for different types of exposure

In this chapter we will consider the approach to developing and implementing hedging strategies. As we have already seen, differing attitudes to risk are likely to mean that hedging strategies will vary from organization to organization. There are, additionally, a number of other factors that can result in different strategies being adopted even where two organizations may have the same degree of risk aversion. These factors relate to the precise nature of the exposures faced and the resources available for managing them. Because these factors will vary considerably from one entity to another, hedging strategies should be developed to meet the particular requirements of the individual organization rather than be imposed rigidly in a manner that assumes that there is only one way to manage each kind of exposure.

The factors that should be considered when developing a hedging strategy are set out below, and are followed by a discussion of the alternative courses of action that could be followed in the management of the more common types of currency exposure. I have assumed, in discussing hedging strategies, that the exposure to be managed is that which remains after all available internal hedging techniques have been implemented.

Developing a hedging strategy

The approach to an organization's hedging strategy will be rooted in its attitude to risk. As we have already discussed in Chapter 3, the foreign exchange policy document should clearly set out the attitude to currency risk and how it is to be managed. These policies should be based on an objective assessment of the nature and significance of the risk that is faced and the resources that the organization is prepared, or can afford, to devote to its management.

Where an organization is very risk averse the policies may set out in detail the cover that must be taken for each type of exposure and the hedging instruments to be used. In less risk averse organizations, the policies may allow the treasury greater freedom to determine the strategy and decide which instrument is the most appropriate for any particular exposure. Overall, hedging strategies tend to fall into the following three broad categories:

● hedge everything (typically in a risk averse cost centre treasury)

- hedge selectively (typically in a value-added service centre treasury), or

- hedge at will (with the aim of maximizing profit, a characteristic of a profit centre treasury).

It is quite possible, and indeed entirely appropriate, that different strategies will be adopted depending upon the following factors.

The type of exposure

The perception of the need to hedge transaction and translation exposures differs from organization to organization and different strategies will therefore be adopted to manage them. Actual exposures may be treated differently from forecast exposures, while contingent exposures, for example, arising from contract tenders, are likely to be managed separately on a case-by-case basis.

Where an exposure arises because a currency price list has been issued, it is likely that a high degree of hedging will take place. If, on the other hand, a currency price is determined by reference to the market rate at the invoice or shipment date, only actual sales may be hedged and the organization may be unconcerned about future exchange rate movements as long as they are not expected to affect its ability to sell its products or trade profitably over the longer term.

The size of the exposures

A large net exposure in a currency or range of currencies will often be viewed as being more necessary to hedge than a small exposure. Where an organization has exposures in a range of currencies but significant exposures in only a few of them (that may, for example, account for 90 per cent of the total), it is likely to concentrate on hedging the main positions and leave the rest unhedged.

The stability of the currencies

If the exchange rate for a currency is very stable compared with another currency, particularly in cases where there is a formal link such as the Exchange Rate Mechanism (ERM), there is considered to be less need to cover exposures. In some cases, forward cover might even result in unfavourable rates being obtained because the effect of the forward premium would be to produce a worse hedge rate than that which could be obtained by arranging a spot contract when the currency receipt or payment is due.

The maturity period of the exposure

It is quite normal for a lower level of cover to be taken out for more distant maturity periods than for nearer ones. This is partly because there is greater uncertainty about the accuracy of exposure forecasts in more distant periods, partly because there is greater uncertainty about exchange rate movements and partly because the perceived cost of cover becomes prohibitive.

Typically, therefore, an organization will not hedge exposures beyond 12 months unless they are commitments and the exchange risk can be clearly defined. Thus, forecasted transaction exposures will either be only partially hedged or not be hedged at all, while a definite commitment to buy a piece of machinery at a fixed currency price for delivery in, say, 18 months' time will normally be covered in order to lock into an approved project cost.

The ability to forecast exposures

If an organization cannot forecast exposures, either because it lacks the resources to do so or because the nature of its overseas business is uncertain, it will be handicapped in its ability to hedge currency risks before they become commitments. In such cases, because it will not have already put in place any cover against future currency flows, it will be fully exposed at the time a commitment is entered into, and would be likely to adopt a strategy of hedging such exposures in full immediately.

The treasury management expertise of the organization

The use of sophisticated hedging instruments and techniques requires a range of treasury management skills that may not be available to many small organizations. Where resources are limited, a fairly basic approach is likely to be taken based on the use of spot and forward foreign exchange contracts and the utilization of any currency balances held on the bank accounts. Hedging strategies are unlikely to involve the use of options or other derivative instruments because these require expertise not only in understanding their use but also in monitoring, reporting and accounting for them.

It is vitally important, if any kind of sophisticated currency option or derivative-based hedging strategy is to be undertaken, that the organization should support the use of such instruments with the ability to value its positions, to decide whether or when to exercise or sell the instruments, to process the instruments through its systems, to generate understandable and accurate management reports and to account for them. It may also, depending upon the organization's tax position, be necessary to understand the tax implications resulting from the use of any particular instrument.

The use of foreign exchange hedging instruments requires the agreement of facilities with bank counterparties. In considering whether to grant such facilities, a bank will be principally concerned with its exposure to the creditworthiness of its counterparty. It is likely, however, that it will also consider the potential size of the foreign exchange business that its customer can offer, the currencies involved, the proposed hedging instruments and the expertise of the customer's staff when deciding whether to set up a dealing relationship.

Access to hedging instruments

A particular bank may decline to offer facilities, or offer only a basic spot and forward foreign exchange line, if it has concerns about creditworthiness; if the volume of business is small; if it does not normally deal in the currencies involved or if it feels that the customer does not have the understanding and expertise to deal in some of the more sophisticated instruments. If an organization does not have access to a wide range of foreign exchange instruments, its hedging strategies will be consequently constrained.

Use of sophisticated hedging instruments and techniques requires a range of treasury management skills not accessible to many small organizations.

Companies are increasingly taking into account the views of their major shareholders with regard to currency risk. A study of the attitudes of institutional shareholders in the UK suggests that, because they themselves have significant Sterling liabilities, their prime concern is that they should receive a strong and consistent Sterling earnings flow from their investments. This suggests that they expect UK corporates to be hedging their currency exposures. A similar view may be taken by institutional shareholders in other countries.

The attitude of shareholders to currency risk

At one end of the scale therefore, one might find a company that uses only spot and forward foreign exchange contracts to manage relatively small currency exposures up to three months out. At the other extreme, a very large multinational company will be using a combination of instruments including currency options and option-based derivatives, to manage significant exposures over a time frame of several years (it may also leave large portions of its forecast exposures unhedged). In between these extremes, there will be a mass of organizations that use a range of instruments to follow a variety of hedging strategies.

Given that, in most organizations, some degree of currency hedging will take place, what approaches are likely to be taken to different kinds of exposure in practice?

Strategies for different kinds of treasury

The risk averse cost centre treasury

In the cost centre treasury the emphasis is on eliminating risk. The typical hedging strategy is therefore to hedge in full all actual (committed) exposures immediately they are identified and, where a high degree of confidence can be placed on the forecast, to hedge significant amounts of uncommitted exposures.

Hedging of transaction exposures is usually effected by means of forward contracts; currency options are not considered appropriate because they imply uncertainty about the underlying risk or the desire to benefit from favourable movements in rates.

Translation exposures are typically hedged by matching assets and liabilities in the same currencies through currency-denominated debt or by creating liabilities through long-term forward contracts. Currency-denominated profits may be hedged by a string of forward contracts put in place each month as the year progresses.

The value-added service centre treasury

The value-added service centre seeks to make a profit contribution by the use of selective hedging within clearly defined parameters. While it is typically required to hedge actual transaction exposures in full, it may do so using currency options as well as more conventional foreign exchange contracts. It tends to have more discretion about whether, and when, to hedge particular exposures, and is often required only to hedge within stated, and fairly wide, percentage bands for particular time periods.

Thus, for forecast transaction exposures, it may be required to have a minimum of, say, 20 per cent and a maximum of 70 per cent cover for a particular future period and wide discretion as to how the cover is effected in terms of the levels by currency and the instruments used.

> In the cost centre treasury the emphasis is on eliminating risk.

Translation exposure may or may not be hedged; many companies that are not particularly risk averse tend to view translation exposure as an accounting rather than a risk management issue. If it is hedged, the standard techniques of matching assets and liabilities will be used and there may also be some use of related currencies to provide proxy hedges.

The profit centre treasury's objective is to make money from currency dealing. Accordingly, it not only manages the currency exposures generated by the organization's underlying business with a view to earning a profit but also creates new exposures with the aim of benefiting from exchange rate movements.

A transaction exposure may therefore be hedged, the hedge closed out to take a gain, and subsequently be rehedged and closed out several times over. Positions may be run, and new ones created through forward contracts or writing options if it is expected that a profit can be made. Profit centre treasuries tend to be the first and most adventurous users of new hedging instruments.

There is usually little emphasis in a profit centre on hedging translation exposures.

Over recent years, a number of surveys in Europe, the USA and Australia have revealed that the great majority of corporate treasuries operate as value-added service centres (even if they use another term to describe themselves). It is in the service centre treasury that what is widely considered an appropriate combination of control with the scope to use technical expertise for the organization's benefit can be found. In the next section of this chapter we will discuss the hedging strategies that a value-added service centre treasury could be expected to adopt towards typical currency exposures.

In the examples we will assume that the value-added service centre treasury is required to carry out a certain minimum amount of hedging for all kinds of exposure and that, above this level, it has discretion whether to hedge or not. For the purposes of the examples we will assume, in each case, that the treasury also has discretion as to the instrument to be used.

Strategies for different types of exposure

Surveys of corporate foreign exchange hedging strategies in a variety of geographical areas indicate that over 95 per cent of companies either fully or partially hedge transaction exposures. Of these companies, approximately one-third fully hedge and two-thirds use selective hedging to manage risk. The most commonly used hedging instrument is the forward contract, which is used by over 90 per cent of companies. Other instruments used are the spot contract (as part of a more complex hedging strategy) by about 80 per cent of companies, currency options and foreign exchange swaps (60 per cent of companies) and currency borrowings by about half of all companies surveyed. Currency futures are used by fewer than 5 per cent of companies.

Actual exposures arise from firm orders or sales for which there is documentary evidence such as an invoice. The amount and payment or receipt date of the currency are fixed and definite. Actual transaction exposures typically mature within three months, except in the case of purchases of capital equipment which tend to have much longer lead times.

Forecast transaction exposures arise from the organization's budgeting or forecasting process and are based on reasonable expectations of future trading activities. In most organizations forecast transaction exposures fall into a four to twelve months' time horizon and are hedged mainly by means of forward contracts; although currency options are increasingly being used in situations where it is expected that exchange rates might move favourably but where it is still necessary to put a hedge in place.

Where a transaction exposure arises in a currency that is subject to exchange restrictions (so that in effect it can only be converted at spot

> *Actual exposures arise from firm orders or sales for which there is documentary evidence.*

rates on presentation of documents), or in which there is a thin market, a hedge may be taken out in a closely related or linked proxy currency. This hedge will then be closed at a later date to realize a currency gain or loss which is then used to offset any movements that have occurred in the exchange rate of the underlying currency.

Another use of proxy currencies is to simplify the hedging process. The ECU, for example, might be hedged as a proxy for a range of European currencies in which there are varying amounts of exposure. One forward contract in the ECU can be executed to cover a number of forecast positions for a particular maturity period. This can then be closed out either at maturity or when the forecasted exposures become firm commitments, a gain or loss realized, and the actual exposures covered with spot or forward contracts. Other examples of proxy currencies are the US Dollar, for a range of Dollar-linked currencies, and the Deutsche Mark for such currencies as the Dutch Guilder and Austrian Schilling.

An alternative to forward cover is to borrow currency and convert into the base currency at spot maturity. Repayments of the borrowing are then made from incoming currency receipts. Alternatively, where payments

Hedging transaction exposures

Potential strategies	Instruments/techniques
Fully hedge using a mixture of forward contracts and currency options to provide flexibility to cater for inaccuracies in forecasting	Forward contract to receipt/payment date
	Forward option contract if there is uncertainty about timing or if a number of small currency flows will take place over a period of time
	Currency put option at-the-money forward for receipts if currency is expected to strengthen
	Currency call option at-the-money forward for payments if currency is expected to weaken
	Buy currency spot and hold on deposit until payment date
	Borrow currency and convert at spot to base currency. Repay borrowing from currency receipts
Partially hedge The degree of cover will depend upon expectations for exchange rate movements. If the currency of exposure is expected to move adversely a higher level of cover will be taken	Forward contracts to receipt payment date to hedge an agreed proportion of exposure
	Forward option contracts for part of the exposure.
	Currency options as above to hedge part of exposure
	Partial currency borrowing/deposit as above
Leave unhedged	Spot deal at maturity

are to be made, the currency could be bought for spot maturity and held on a currency bank account on deposit until it is used to pay creditors. There are, of course, interest costs associated with managing exposure in this way as opposed to incurring the cost of the forward premium or discount. Currency borrowings and deposits tend to be used by organizations that require flexibility over the amounts and timings of currency flows and which may not have access to the facilities to arrange forward contracts.

Contingent transaction exposures

These will arise, for example, when a tender has been submitted for a contract that will result, if won, in currency receipts or payments. Because it is uncertain, at the time the tender is submitted, whether the contract will be won it is necessary if the contingent exposure is to be hedged to do so in a way that does not create a commitment to deliver or take delivery of currency. For this reason, most tender situations are hedged by means of currency options or other option-based derivatives. As we have seen, the longer the maturity period of an option is the more expensive is the premium cost. Because of this, it is important to identify accurately the period of uncertainty that is to be hedged.

A typical tendering situation will involve the following elements:

- the amount of the currency receipts and/or payments that will result if the tender is successful
- the timing of those receipts and payments
- the date for the submission of the tender, and
- the date on which the winner of the contract is announced.

> *It is important to identify accurately the period of uncertainty that is to be hedged.*

The period of uncertainty to be hedged is the time between the submission of the tender and the announcement of the winner of the contract. The total amount of the flows should be hedged but the timing of the currency flows that will arise from the contract is, at the tender date, irrelevant.

An organization that is tendering for a contract will normally take out some form of option or option-based cover. This should be for the period from when the tender is submitted to the date on which it will know whether it has won the contract or not. At the time at which the result of the tender is announced, two things need to be considered.

These are the value, if any, of the tender hedge and the need, if any, to take out any further hedging. Whether the organization has won the contract or not, its hedge may have intrinsic value that can be realized. If there is intrinsic value, the option should be exercised or sold. If there is no intrinsic value, the option will lapse.

If it has won the contract, the organization can then take out further cover in the form of forward contracts, currency options, cylinder options or some other appropriate derivative. If exchange rates have moved adversely since the tender date, the tender hedge will have yielded an exchange gain which will offset the effect of the worse rates that are now applicable to the contract hedge. If, on the other

> *An organization tendering for a contract will normally take out an option or option-based cover.*

hand, exchange rates have moved favourably between the tender date and the award of the contract, the tender hedge would have no value but the new hedges of the flows arising from the contract will be arranged at better rates and the organization will benefit from this.

Hedging contingent exposures

Potential hedging strategies	Instruments
Fully or partially hedge contingent exposure	Currency option from tender date to contract award date
	Tender to contract cover (TTC)
	Shared currency option, under tender (SCOUT)

Translation exposure

Surveys indicate that about one-third of companies do not hedge translation exposures at all, while half undertake only partial hedging. The main reason for there being less interest in hedging translation exposure than transaction exposure is that it is seen largely as a book-keeping, non-cash issue that does not justify the implementation of hedging actions that use bank facilities and require administrative effort to manage them. Where translation exposure is hedged, the most common techniques used are currency borrowings and forward contracts. There appears to be more emphasis on hedging translation exposure in smaller companies, where certainty of results is often considered to be more important than in larger organizations.

As noted above, the two most commonly used techniques for managing translation exposure are currency borrowings and forward contracts to match net currency assets. In each case, the result is to create a currency liability that offsets a net balance sheet position in currency, and thereby eliminates the exposure. If currency borrowings are used therefore, they should be used to acquire the currency-denominated asset or, if the assets have already been acquired, converted into the organization's base currency. When forward contracts are used to hedge translation exposure, they must be taken out for long maturities. It is not uncommon for forward contracts maturing in five or more years' time to be used.

Other instruments that are used to hedge translation exposure are foreign exchange swaps, currency options and, by a very small minority of companies, currency futures. As with transaction exposure, there is some use of proxy currencies in the management of translation exposure. This can work in two ways; where there are offsetting positions in linked currencies (for example, the Deutsche Mark and the Dutch Guilder) these are regarded as hedging each other and no further action is taken; alternatively, where there is a balance sheet exposure in a currency that perhaps because of exchange restrictions or other controls would be difficult to hedge directly, a hedge could be constructed against a linked, convertible currency.

Hedging translation exposures

Potential hedging strategy	Instruments/techniques
Fully or partially hedge net assets	Currency borrowing in same currency
	Currency borrowing in proxy currency
	Forward contracts in same currency
	Forward contracts in proxy currency
	Matching of offsetting position in proxy or related currency
	Foreign exchange swaps
	Currency options
	Currency futures

Approximately two-thirds of companies claim to hedge foreign-currency-denominated profits. Traditionally, the most common technique used to do this has been to sell each month's profit forward against the group base currency using forward contracts maturing at the company's year end. On maturity, the contracts are closed out and a gain or loss realized to offset the effects of exchange rate movements over the year. The objective of this exercise is to achieve an average exchange rate for the translation of profits as they are earned throughout the year.

With the introduction of more sophisticated option-based derivatives increasing use of instruments like the average rate option has been seen in the hedging of currency profits. As discussed in Chapter 5, the average rate option allows the purchaser to buy or sell currency at the average market rate that prevailed in a given period. This instrument allows a more genuinely average rate to be achieved than that obtained by a forward contract that is fixed on one particular date in the month.

Hedging currency-denominated profits

Potential strategy	Instruments/techniques
Fully or partially hedge	Forward contracts
	Average rate options

The approach to an organization's hedging strategy should be based on its attitude to risk. The degree of hedging that is carried out will be greatest in the most risk averse entities and hedging strategies will therefore be more demanding.

The hedging strategy adopted will depend on a number of factors, including:

- the type of exposure
- the size of the exposures
- the stability of the currencies
- the maturity periods of the exposures
- the ability to forecast exposures
- the treasury management expertise of the organization
- access to hedging instruments, and
- the attitude of shareholders.

Part Three

**The approach taken
to dealing can make
a big difference
to the effectiveness
of an organization's
foreign exchange
management
operations.**

7

Dealing procedures and market conventions

- Dealing procedures
- Market conventions

Dealing procedures

···

The approach taken to dealing can make a big difference to the effectiveness of an organization's foreign exchange management operations. A well thought out routine will not only enable elementary mistakes to be avoided, it will also allow the organization to project a professional image to bank counterparties. This can be very important in getting the best possible rates.

A suggested approach to dealing includes the following steps.

Deal identification procedures
·······················

The need to transact a foreign exchange deal will be recognized in a number of ways and it is, of course, essential to be able to validate, as far as possible, that the exposure exists or, in the case of a forecasted exposure, is reasonably likely to arise.

Exposures may be recognized by the treasury function by means of:

- written requests for cover received from subsidiaries. These should set out the currency to be bought or sold, the amount of the transaction, the maturity date and settlement instructions. These should be in a standard format to ensure that all essential information is provided. Where a large number of transactions are carried out for a particular subsidiary, each request should carry a sequential reference number to assist deal identification. The company should ensure that such written requests are signed by specified authorized signatories

- output from the currency netting analysis (whether produced manually or by a computer program) using actual and forecast exposure data provided by subsidiaries

- other information sources including the treasury's own data. The sort of exposures that will be included in this category are intercompany dividend payments, interest and principal payments on foreign currency debt and transactions required to manage translation exposure.

Having received a request to hedge or recognized an exposure the treasury activity should proceed in the following way.

All hedging requests from subsidiaries should be checked to confirm that they are properly authorized and in conformity with approved policies and controls. Authorization might be required internally if the size or maturity period of the deal or the proposed hedging instrument requires the approval of the treasurer, finance director or other officer before the dealer can arrange the transaction.

Satisfy deal authority requirements

The deal must also, of course, conform with the terms of the mandates issued to the banks and dealing facilities provided by the banks, otherwise it will either be in breach of the mandates or simply not possible to arrange.

As discussed in Chapter 3, the banks with which the organization deals should be limited to a pre-determined list of authorized counterparties. From these, the treasury should select the bank or banks which it will ask to quote on a transaction according to its estimation of the likely source of the best rates. In doing this, it will consider a number of factors, including the two currencies involved in the deal. A basic rule of thumb here is that a bank that is based in the country of one or other of the currencies is likely to be the most competitive seller of that currency as it will have a natural position (and often a cheap source, especially if it is a clearing bank) in the currency. Thus, if a British company wished to buy French Francs against Sterling, it should ask the London entity of at least one French bank to quote for the business as well as approaching a British clearing bank.

Select appropriate banks to be asked to quote

Other factors which may influence the choice of bank are the size of the deal (some banks are better than others in quoting for particularly large or small amounts), the maturity of the deal, the type of hedging instrument (some banks are not active dealers in derivatives), the speed with which the bank normally provides a quote, the efficiency of the bank in

The organization should have a pre-determined list of authorized banks with which it deals.

confirming and settling transactions, the company's relationship with the bank's staff and even whether the two parties have recently discussed how they can do more business with each other.

Having selected possible banks to be asked to quote, the treasury should, of course, check that there is enough unutilized limit available with each bank for the deal to be arranged without breaching the company's counterparty limits.

It is important to remember that, although great care may have been taken in selecting banks that are most likely to offer competitive quotes, the company cannot know exactly what a bank's position is in a particular currency at the time that it wishes to deal. It may happen that a bank will give an uncompetitive quote because the deal did not suit its own position; it may have already been long in the currency that its customer was trying to sell. If a bank finds itself in the position of having to quote an uncompetitive rate, it will often decline to quote rather than be seen to offer a poor rate. This saves both sides the time and effort of an unrealistic and (probably) losing quote and enables the company to contact another bank which may be eager to do the deal.

In some circumstances, however, it may be advantageous not to obtain competitive quotes; particularly for forward deals or broken dates. The reason for this is that a bank will normally try to cover or 'lay off' its position in the market when dealing with a corporate. If the transaction is a large one and for an unusual maturity date, the effect of competitive quoting will be to multiply the position in the market and to move the price against the company. For example, a deal to buy 50 million Australian Dollars that has been quoted to three banks will appear to the market as a demand for 150 million Australian Dollars, and it is likely that there will be an immediate strengthening of the AUD before the deal can be completed. The effect, therefore, is that the company will have moved the market against itself. In such circumstances it may be better to go to one bank that is known to be a major player in the currency and to ask them to quote on the basis that the deal is not competitive. The bank's dealer can then offer a keen price, knowing that the other banks in the market are not aware of the transaction and that they are therefore unlikely to move rates against him while he is arranging the deal. The company can, of course, always check the rate offered by the bank against those shown on its electronic market information system if it wishes to confirm that the bank is genuinely quoting a market price.

The treasury should keep records of the transactions that each bank has been asked to quote for and the rates offered so that it can assess objectively over time which banks are most competitive for particular types of transaction. The more sophisticated treasury systems allow this to be done automatically.

Timing the deal

Having identified which banks it will ask to quote on the deal, the treasury needs to consider when the best time to deal might be. There may not, of course, be a choice. It may be necessary to hedge immediately because spot settlement is required or because the company's treasury policies require an identified exposure to be covered without delay.

If the policies allow the treasury to choose when to deal, it should consider whether the exchange rate is expected to move in a favourable direction and whether a better rate might possibly be obtained if dealing were delayed by an hour, a day or a week. If it is decided that the exposure will not

The treasury needs to consider when the best time to deal might be.

be hedged immediately, this should only be done after considering the financial, economic and political factors that are expected to affect the currency or currencies involved and canvassing a representative and reasonably well-informed range of views in the foreign exchange market and internally within the company.

The company should also consider the point of view of the banks when it is deciding when to transact a deal. As noted above, banks normally lay off a deal to cover their position; this is typically done either with a broker or directly with a foreign bank. This may involve the bank's dealer contacting a bank in the country of the currency, or in the USA, as well as a broker. The time of day at which the deal is done will determine how many of the above options are available to the bank. Banks in London will only be able to deal with banks in the Arabian Gulf in the morning (and not at all on Fridays) and banks in the USA in the afternoon. Banks in Scandinavia finish dealing in mid-afternoon London time and those on the Continent close earlier than London.

A bank will not be eager to deal if it cannot lay off its position quickly. Asking for quotes in Saudi Rials on a Thursday afternoon or Swedish Krona on a Friday afternoon, when these currencies cannot be laid off until the following Monday, is likely to result in being offered rates that include a wide spread as an insurance against any adverse market movements before the deal is laid off with another bank.

The best approach, to avoid this problem, is to deal when the foreign exchange markets in the country of the currencies are open or, if this is not possible, to ensure that the US market is open.

When it is ready to deal, the treasury should ensure that it understands the transaction. This may sound obvious, but it is by no means unknown for dealers to make a mistake and buy the currency they should be selling, trade the wrong amount or deal for the wrong value date. A few seconds spent in understanding the transaction will enable these kinds of mistake to be avoided.

Understand the deal

Estimate the expected rate
....

The dealers should also assess what rate they expect to be quoted. This is easy if the treasury has an on-line market information system, such as that provided by Reuters. Spot rates supplied by a variety of banks are shown on the system and constantly updated. Outright forward rates are either shown on the system or can be calculated by adjusting the spot rates by the relevant forward points.

> *The treasury should ensure that it understands the transaction.*

It is essential that the dealer should have a reasonable idea of what rate the bank should quote, otherwise it will not know if the bank has made a mistake (they sometimes do) or is offering a very poor rate. It may deliberately quote an off-market rate if the deal does not suit its book or if it perceives that its customer does not know what the correct market level is. If it does not have an on-line information system, the treasury should be careful not to act in a way that will alert its banks to its lack of market rate information to avoid the risk of being taken advantage of through its ignorance of current market rates. Competitive quoting of two banks simultaneously will provide some protection against bank errors or off-market quotes as it is unlikely that both banks will be equally prone to error or in the same position *vis-à-vis* the market, but there will still be a risk that the banks will not quote the most competitive rates.

If the transaction is in an unusual currency pair or one that the company is not familiar with, the treasury should ensure that it knows which way round the rate will be quoted and whether the better rate is the higher or lower of two competing quotes. This will depend on the currencies being dealt and whether the company is buying or selling. For example:

Example Swedish Krona (SEK) versus Portuguese Escudo (PTE) transaction

➤ **Is the rate quoted Escudos per Krona or Krona per Escudo?**

Spot rates against the US Dollar:

Escudo   156.105
Swedish Krona   6.7361

Cross rate is therefore SEK 1 = PTE 23.1744

➤ **Which is the better rate for selling Escudos or selling Krona?**

For selling PTE the lowest rate (fewest PTE paid) is best
For selling SEK the highest rate (most PTE bought) is best

Before the banks are contacted, the treasury should partially complete a **Enter deal details** deal ticket for the deal, entering the currencies to be bought and sold, the **on the deal ticket** amount to be either bought or sold, the maturity date, the names of the banks to be quoted, the entity on whose behalf the deal is to be done (this will either be the group treasury or a subsidiary depending upon the company's organizational arrangements), the reason for the deal and settlement instructions. An example of a deal ticket is shown at the end of Chapter 8. The example shown is designed for spot and forward contracts; currency option and other derivative contracts would require a different format to cater for the specific needs of the instrument. The example deal ticket also shows how the control process for electronic payment of a Sterling amount in settlement of a purchase of currency can be set out on the deal ticket. This concept can, of course, be used for any currency in which a transfer from the company's bank accounts is required to effect settlement. If the treasury operates a 'paperless dealing room' the details of the deal should be entered directly onto the treasury computer system.

Each dealer should have a copy of the deal details before contact is made with the bank.

Each dealer should have a copy of the details of the deal before contact is made with the banks so that he or she can fully understand the transaction before the banks are contacted.

The next step is to contact the selected banks. If the deal is to be dealt **Telephone the** competitively, it is essential to contact both banks at the same time and **banks** give them the details of the deal simultaneously. This will normally require the use of two dealers.

If one bank is asked to quote before the other, it is almost impossible to ensure that both banks are quoting comparable rates, particularly if the market is volatile. The dealer is likely to have a rate from the first bank quoted but not from the second bank and then when the second bank quotes to find that the first bank is changing its quote. This can easily develop into a situation in which the treasury never manages to have two quotes at the same time, and each new quote is worse than the previous one. In such a situation it may be best to abandon the deal and try again later.

The way in which the details of a deal are given to the bank can minimize **Dealing** the risk of confusion and assist the bank to give the best quote in the shortest possible time. In essence, the dealer should give all of the necessary information as succinctly and clearly as possible. The information required is:

- who the dealer and the company are. This enables the bank to verify that the dealer is authorized
- the entity in whose name the deal is to be transacted
- the kind of deal to be arranged (spot, forward, purchased currency option, etc)
- the maturity date
- the currency to be bought and the currency to be sold, and
- the amount of the bought or sold currency (at this stage you will only know the amount to be *either* bought *or* sold).

It is also worth letting the bank know if the deal is being quoted competitively. It should be noted that it is now standard practice for banks to tape record all dealing conversations (many corporate treasuries also do this). This is useful in resolving disputes or misunderstandings if they arise. In view of this, it is important that the corporate dealer should speak clearly and unambiguously to the bank.

The conversation with the bank might run as follows:

Company dealer: *"Good morning, this is John Smith of the XYZ plc treasury department, I would like to arrange a foreign exchange transaction in the name of our subsidiary, ABC Limited. Can you give me a competitive quote, please?"*

Bank dealer: *"Good morning John, this is Steve, certainly I can show you a rate. What are the details of the deal?"*

Company dealer: *"I would like you to quote me for a forward contract maturing on 20 June. I buy twenty million French Francs and sell you Sterling."*

An alternative approach is to ask for a two-way price; that is, for a quote both to buy and sell the currency. The drawback with this is that the bank is likely to quote less competitive rates if it does not know whether it will be buying or selling the currency.

Bank dealer: *"OK, You want me to sell you twenty million French Francs and buy your Sterling for value 20 June. That's approximately three months forward. Just a second, I'll get you a rate."*

"The spot is 7.7830, I'm just waiting for the forward points."

"The forward points are 345 against you."

Company dealer: *"That makes the outright 7.7485. Just a moment, I'm waiting for my other bank."*

The other bank gives a quote of 7.7484 and the company's other dealer rejects its quote by saying, *"Sorry, no deal, but thanks very much for your quote"* to make it absolutely clear that it has not won the deal.

Often the bank dealer will want to know how close he was to winning the deal or whether his quote was very uncompetitive. He might ask, *"How far off were we on that one?"* The company will often find it difficult to answer this as its answer can affect the relationship with the bank and its competitiveness in the future: if it says the bank was very close to winning, it fears that this will not encourage the bank to try harder to be more competitive next time. If, on the other hand, it says that the bank was way off the market it may not be believed. The company dealer may simply say something vague like *"you were a few points out."*

If both banks offer the same quote, the company would normally do the deal with the bank that was quickest to quote as a reward for efficiency, unless there was a particular reason that it wanted to do the deal with the other bank. The company might do this if it wants to show that it is using facilities provided by the bank, if it is trying to build up a relationship or if settlement is easier with one bank rather than another one.

Company dealer: *"OK, that's done at 7.7485. I buy twenty million French Francs and sell you Sterling at a rate of 7.7485 for value 30 June. Can we agree the Sterling amount? I make it £2 581 144 spot 70".*

Bank dealer: *"OK, I sell you twenty million French Francs against Sterling for value 30 June at 7.7485. I agree the Sterling of £2 581 144 spot 70. My back office will contact you later to confirm details and settlement. Thanks very much for your business:.*

Company dealer: *"Thanks very much, goodbye."*

When the deal has been completed, it must be recorded and confirmed without delay and arrangements must also be in place to ensure that when it matures, which could be at a distant future date, action is taken to settle, close out or roll the transaction.

Completion of the deal ticket

The primary record of every transaction is the deal ticket. It can now be completed by adding the winning rate and the competitive quote offered, the Sterling amount paid for the French Francs and the settlement details for the Sterling. The dealer should then sign the deal ticket.

Before passing the deal ticket to the back office for processing, the dealer also records the details of the deal in his diary on the page for the deal maturity date and on the page for the spot value date, which is normally two working days before maturity. He notes the impending maturity on the spot value date because, if the deal is to be closed out or rolled over to a later date, this will have to be done (for most currencies) no later than the spot value date. If, on the other hand, the company will want to take delivery of the currency purchased, payment instructions should be provided to the bank by the spot value date to enable settlement to be made by the maturity date.

> The primary record of every transaction is the deal ticket.

If the dealing room is 'paperless', the details of the deal will be input by the dealer directly to the computer system and the company's records will be immediately updated. The back office will then take responsibility for further administration of the transaction.

Deal processing

If the treasury does not operate a 'paperless' dealing room, the deal ticket should be passed by the dealer to a separate back office or administration function so that:

- the deal can be recorded in the treasury computer system
- a confirmation of the deal can be produced and sent to the counterparty
- the deal can be settled on the maturity date by appropriate funds transfers
- information can be produced for accounting purposes, and
- management reports can be generated.

All of these actions rely on the information that is recorded on the deal ticket; this underlines the importance of the deal ticket as a primary document and the need to ensure that every transaction is recorded fully and accurately. A key control mechanism to ensure that deal tickets do not get lost, or escape from the system in any other way, is the sequential pre-numbering of the tickets. The back office should ensure that it has an unbroken sequence of deal tickets, including any that may have been spoilt, so that it can verify that all recorded deals have been recognized by the system, confirmed and accounted for.

The majority of corporate treasuries use treasury management computer systems to record and process their dealing transactions. These systems fall into two broad categories: 'off the shelf' packages marketed by specialist suppliers and bespoke systems developed exclusively for the user. While package systems tend to have relatively standard features and be designed to run on IBM compatible PCs, bespoke systems can range from simple spreadsheets to complex systems running on the company's mainframe computer. Those companies that do not have computer-based systems for deal processing usually keep manual records and prepare confirmation letters on an *ad hoc* basis using a standard format on a word processing package.

Deal recording

The objectives of deal recording are to ensure that all deals are:

- **Confirmed in writing with the counterparty**

Every transaction should be confirmed in writing with the counterparty as soon as possible after the deal is struck. The confirmation letter should be signed by two authorized signatories, one of whom should be the treasurer or assistant treasurer and the other someone who does not work in the treasury. The deal ticket and any supporting documentation that is available to explain or validate the transaction should be provided to the signatories so that they can check both that the confirmation reflects the details recorded on the deal ticket and that they understand the reason for the transaction. Signatories to deal confirmation letters are typically the same personnel as cheque signatories. A key function of the confirmation letter is to act as a statement to the counterparty of the company's understanding of the transaction. If the company has for any reason recorded the details erroneously, this can then be identified and resolved with the bank as early as possible rather than being discovered when the deal matures.

If the transaction is a spot deal, it is likely that the confirmation letter will include settlement instructions. Settlement is likely to be to:

- a bank account held by a company within the group. If a subsidiary has purchased currency for payment to a supplier, it may initially take the currency into its own bank account and subsequently pay it away from the account. This is generally recognized as the most secure means of settlement; or

- a third party; the bank may be instructed to pay the funds directly to a supplier's bank account. This is likely to happen in cases where the company does not hold a bank account in the currency concerned or when an urgent payment is required; or

- another bank. This could occur when a maturing contract with one bank is closed out by a purchase of currency from another bank or where the currency is needed to repay a borrowing or to pay interest on a borrowing. The bank from which the currency is bought is instructed to pay direct to the other bank for its account, 'in favour of' or 'reference' the name of the company. At the same time, the company would advise the bank of its receipt of funds and which bank will be delivering them.

If the transaction is a forward deal and the company does not, at the moment, know the payment instructions or expects that the deal may eventually be rolled over to a later date, it will not be able to, or may decide not to, provide payment instructions with the deal confirmation. In such a case, payment instructions may not be provided to the bank until the actual time of settlement.

A specimen deal confirmation letter is shown at the end of Chapter 8.

- **Settled on maturity**

A foreign exchange contract creates a binding commitment to both deliver and receive currency on the maturity date (even if this is achieved by closing out the original contract or rolling it over to a later maturity date). This being the case, it is vital that the company's transaction records correctly identify and give adequate warning of maturing contracts. This is particularly important if forward contracts maturing several years ahead are entered into, as these may not have been logged in the dealer's diary at the date of inception and, indeed, the treasury staff responsible may have left the company before the deals mature.

Treasury computer systems are particularly useful in identifying maturing transactions as they typically have a maturity diary capability that lists all deals maturing within a future time period selected by the user. Most corporate treasuries produce a report of this kind from their systems each day to list the deals maturing within the next week or month.

If manual records are maintained, the company must be very diligent in updating the maturity listing every time a deal is arranged. Maturities for the year ahead should be entered into the dealer's diary as soon as it is available.

Settlement of maturing transactions must be carried out within a tightly controlled environment that satisfies the requirements set out in Chapter 8 for the prevention of fraud. Each maturing transaction involves two movements of funds (except where a deal is closed out with the original bank, in which case there is only one movement of funds in respect of the balance due either to the bank or the

A foreign exchange contract creates a binding commitment to deliver and receive currency on the maturity date.

company). It is essential to control both the payment to the bank of the currency sold to it and the payment by the bank of the currency purchased from it. The key tools for exercising the necessary control are the bank mandates and, where relevant, the password, access and physical controls over any electronic funds transfer system that may be used. The control environment is discussed in detail in the following chapter.

- **Included in the organization's accounting records**

Transaction details can be entered into the accounting records in a variety of ways. Some of the most common routes depend upon the provision of information on a deal by deal basis to the accounting function. This may take the form of:

- copies of deal confirmation letters
- print-outs of summaries of transactions obtained from the treasury computer system, and
- direct electronic transfers of information from the treasury system to the accounting system through an interface.

Alternatively, the treasury may account for its own transactions and provide ledger entries to the accounting function.

It is usually considered desirable, from a control point of view, for treasury accounting to be performed outside the treasury and to be based on records of individual transactions so that the accounts department can maintain full control over, and understanding of, entries to the accounts.

- **Monitored by senior management**

The signing process for the confirmation letter enables the company to monitor the actions of the dealer on a day to day basis by reviewing the transactions that are being entered into, and the bank counterparties used. This acts as a basic check that exposures are being hedged in accordance with policies, strategies and forecasts, that authorized hedging instruments and authorized banks are used and that deals are within the approved counterparty limits.

● **Reconcilable with external documents**

It is common practice for a copy of the company's confirmation letter to be provided to the accounting function and for reconciliation with incoming counterparty confirmations and bank statements to be performed against it. Reconciliation is a key control as it is the means by which transactions that have not been recorded in the company's systems can be identified and discrepancies between the company's and the banks' records can be resolved.

● **Included in management reports**

A common feature of treasury systems, both bespoke and package, is that they can be used to produce management reports based on the transaction data that have been input to them. Package systems are particularly flexible in this regard as most systems enable the users to design their own report formats to suit individual needs. The use of a treasury computer system enables a database of transactions and bank performance to be built up over the course of time. This database can be used to generate useful comparative analyses for measuring the performance of the treasury and its dealings with its relationship banks. In order to create a database for analyzing bank performance, it is necessary to input not only the details of transactions that have been dealt with counterparties but also the losing quotes offered by competing banks.

Clearly, computer generated reporting enables a wide range of reports to be produced, facilitates *ad hoc* reporting, minimizes the time required for analysis and typing, and eliminates the risk of calculation and transcription errors. Such reporting does, of course, depend upon comprehensive and accurate input of transaction details in the first place.

If manual records are kept or deals are recorded on spreadsheets, it is less easy to manipulate data for reporting purposes, only relatively basic reports tend to be produced and meaningful analyses comparing one period with another can be particularly difficult to prepare.

Treasury systems The description above of the procedure to follow in dealing and deal processing referred to a variety of electronic systems that may be used by the treasury to facilitate the process. Over recent years the capabilities of these systems have been subject to continuous improvement and the competition for the supply of these services has intensified. This has resulted in a number of benefits for treasury managers, which include the following treasury management tools.

● **Balance reporting and electronic funds transfer services**

Balance reporting systems enable corporate treasurers to identify on a daily basis the positions on their bank accounts around the world. This information is essential to the effective management of currency balances and, of course, to the control of interest income and expense. Balance and transaction reporting systems with international coverage are provided by a number of major banks.

Funds transfer systems enable the instructions authorizing the transmission of funds to be transmitted to banks electronically, rather than by letter, telephone, telex or fax. The main benefits of electronic funds transfer are the increased security over transfer instructions and the speed with which verified instructions can be provided to the banks. These features are particularly valuable where the alternative methods of providing instructions are by letter or telephone.

Both balance reporting and funds transfer systems are well protected by password access.

Where a pre-defined list of payees can be established, as, for example, with a corporate's authorized counterparties, these can be set up as standing data on the system to minimize the time and risk of error involved in entering transfer instructions. This feature also enhances the control environment because it is also possible to restrict transfers to the defined counterparties.

Both balance reporting and funds transfer systems are well protected by password access and activities within the systems can be separated to allow specified individuals to perform particular functions. This is particularly important in the case of funds transfer and it is a standard feature of such systems that the actions of input, verification and release are strictly segregated.

Access to the banks' systems is typically effected by means of a modem link.

● **Market rate and financial information**

The information available from these systems can be tailored to some extent to the users' requirements, thereby enabling the customer to minimize the cost of the service. Up-to-date market information is supplied constantly by a large number of market participants so that an objective picture can be obtained at all times of the rates available in the market. This information is invaluable in identifying both what the rate for any particular transaction should be and which banks are offering the most competitive quotes at any time.

- **A range of modular treasury management systems**

These systems enable treasurers to establish a database of transaction and exposure information which is used both for processing deals (for example, the production of confirmation letters, settlement instructions, accounting data and management reporting) and for performing analysis of potential hedging and other risk management strategies. The majority of systems are PC based and all incorporate control features that enable access to the system, and particular functions within the system, to be segregated in line with the segregation of duties established within the treasury function.

- **Complex software for decision support, option pricing and risk management**

There are a number of software packages available for modelling and comparing different hedging strategies, pricing currency options, valuing hedging portfolios, and so on.

Market conventions

An understanding of the most common market conventions will assist a treasury dealer to project a professional image when dealing and, in doing so, improve the chance of obtaining the most competitive rate for a deal. Some basic market conventions are set out below.

- Currencies are normally quoted as so many units per US Dollar. For example, quotes will be expressed in terms of so many Deutsche Marks to the Dollar (at the time of writing there are approximately 1.53 Deutsche Marks to the Dollar), so many French Francs and so on, rather than saying that 1 Deutsche Mark buys 65 US cents.

- Cross rates are normally calculated by taking the rates for two currencies against the Dollar, although some banks do employ cross rate dealers for key currency pairs. The rate for Yen against the French Franc would therefore be calculated by taking the Dollar/Yen rate and dividing it by the French Franc/Dollar rate, in the following way:

Dollar/Yen rate	105.725
divided by	
Dollar/French Franc	5.1585
equals	
Yen/French Franc rate	20.495

- A bank will give a 'two way' quote – both the bid and offer (or buy and sell) rates – unless the customer states whether he is buying or selling the currency. The difference between the two rates is the bank's spread, or profit margin.

- The spread is expressed in terms of 'pips' or 'points'. Thus the bid/offer spread on a spot of $1.5300/1.5310 is ten points. $1.5300 would, incidentally, be quoted as '$1.53 the figure'.

- When transacting a forward deal, it is normal practice for the bank to quote the spot rate and then the forward points, rather than an outright forward rate. Typically one would agree (or 'fix') the spot rate on which the forward points are to be based before dealing on the forward points. This is because the spot element in a forward rate is the more volatile part of the rate and therefore should be fixed before the forward points are calculated. Fixing the spot rate does not imply that the customer is committed to transacting the forward deal with the bank, it is simply a means of calculating a forward rate. Until the customer has been quoted both elements of the rate – the spot and the forward points – he does not know which of two competing quotes will be the better one and therefore cannot commit himself.

  The reason for this is made clear in the following example:

➤ **A company wishes to buy French Francs against Sterling maturing in three months' time. It asks two banks to quote for a forward contract.**   **Example**

Bank A quotes a spot rate of 7.7525
Bank B quotes a spot rate of 7.7527

➤ **At this stage, Bank B appears to be more competitive but the company cannot commit to the deal until it knows what the forward points will be.**

Bank A quotes forward points of 460 'against you' to produce an outright rate of 7.7065
Bank B quotes forward points of 463 to produce an outright rate of 7.7064

➤ **When the forward points are taken into account Bank A has quoted the better rate and wins the deal.**

● The foreign exchange market prefers to deal in both large and round amounts. The rate for a small transaction can be expected to be less competitive than that for a large amount. In this context, amounts of $5 million and upwards are considered to be marketable amounts that will attract the keenest rates. Similarly, banks prefer to deal in round five or ten million amounts that are easy to cover elsewhere in the market rather than odd amounts. A company treasurer will, of course, have little opportunity to package foreign exchange transactions in round amounts but should attempt to maximize the size of any individual deal, consistent with taking advantage of opportunities to net off two way currency flows.

● Straight dates and broken dates can affect the competitiveness of the rate quoted. On each dealing day there is a recognized spot, one month, two months, three months forward date, and so on. A maturity date that falls on the appropriate forward date for that dealing day is known as a 'straight date'; any other date is known as a 'broken date'. In a highly competitive market, a customer could expect to receive a finer rate for a straight date than for a broken date as a straight date is more likely to suit a bank's 'book' or position.

> *The foreign exchange market prefers to deal in both large and round amounts.*

● When confirming a foreign exchange transaction and giving settlement instructions, it is advisable to use either the full names or the generally recognized abbreviations for the currencies involved. The markets have standardized on the codes established by the Society for Worldwide Interbank Financial Telecommunication (SWIFT). Use of these codes should reduce the risk of misunderstandings and problems with settlement. A list of SWIFT codes for the more commonly traded currencies is shown at the end of this chapter.

● Like many professions and trades, foreign exchange dealers tend to use a lot of slang and abbreviations (partly because of the time constraints imposed by dealing). A corporate dealer should try to learn, and where appropriate use, the same language as the bank dealers. Common slang for major currencies includes 'cable' for the US Dollar/Sterling rate (originating from the undersea trans-Atlantic cable that carried market information between Britain and the US), 'Paris' for the French Franc and 'Swissy' for the Swiss Franc.

The glossary of terms at the end of this book lists and explains most of the market terminology and slang that the corporate dealer is likely to encounter when dealing with banks.

Summary

The approach taken to dealing can make a big difference to an organization's foreign exchange management operations. The right procedures can enable mistakes to be avoided and a professional image to be projected. This can assist in obtaining the best possible rates.

An outline recommended approach to dealing includes the following steps:

- establish efficient deal identification procedures
- ensure that deal authorization requirements are satisfied
- select appropriate banks
- time the deal to enhance the opportunity of obtaining the best rate
- understand the transaction
- estimate the expected rate
- enter deal details on a deal ticket
- provide all necessary information and be clear and concise when dealing
- record full details on the deal ticket, and complete deal recording, confirmation and settlement procedures after dealing.

It is important, also, to understand foreign exchange market conventions and dealing terminology to be able to appear professional when talking to the banks.

A list of SWIFT codes for the more commonly traded currencies

Country	Currency	Code	Country	Currency	Code
Argentina	Peso	ARA	Jamaica	Jamaican Dollar	JMD
Aruba	Aruban Florin	AWG	Japan	Yen	JPY
Austria	Schilling	ATS	Kenya	Kenyan Shilling	KES
Australia	Australian Dollar	AUD	Kuwait	Kuwaiti Dinar	KWD
Bahamas	Bahamian Dollar	BSD	Lesotho	Loti	LSL
Barbados	Barbados Dollar	BBD	Mauritius	Mauritius Rupee	MUR
Bahrain	Bahraini Dinar	BDI	Malaysia	Ringgit	MYR
Belgium	Belgian Franc	BEF	Malawi	Kwacha	MWK
Belize	Belize Dollar	BZD	Mexico	Peso	MXP
Bermuda	Bermudian Dollar	BMD	Netherlands Antilles	Antilles Guilder	ANG
Botswana	Pula	BWP			
Brazil	Cruzeiro Real	BRC	Netherlands	Guilder	NLG
Brazil	New Cruzeiro	NCR	New Zealand	New Zealand Dollar	NZD
Bulgaria	Lev	BGL			
Canada	Canadian Dollar	CAD	Nigeria	Naira	NGN
Cayman Islands	Cayman Islands Dollar	KYD	Norway	Norwegian Krone	NOK
			Poland	Zloty	PLZ
China	Yuan Renminbi	CNY	Portugal	Escudo	PTE
Cyprus	Cyprus Pound	CYP	Russia	Rouble	RUR
Czech Republic	Coruna	CZK	Saudi Arabia	Saudi Rial	SAR
Denmark	Danish Krone	DKK	Seychelles	Rupee	SCR
East Caribbean	East Caribbean Dollar	XCD	Sierra Leone	Leone	SLL
			Singapore	Singapore Dollar	SGD
European Currency Unit	European Currency Unit	XEU	South Africa	Rand	ZAR
			South Korea	Won	KRW
Fiji Islands	Fiji Dollar	FJD	Spain	Peseta	ESP
Finland	Markka	FIM	Swaziland	Lilangeni	SZL
France	French Franc	FRF	Sweden	Swedish Krona	SEK
Germany	Deutsche Mark	DEM	Switzerland	Swiss Franc	CHF
Ghana	Cedi	GHC	Taiwan	Taiwan Dollar	TWD
Gibraltar	Gibraltar Pound	GIP	Tanzania	Shilling	TAN
Greece	Drachma	GRD	Trinidad and Tobago	Trinidad and Tobago Dollar	TTD
Guyana	Guyanese Dollar	GYD			
Hong Kong	Hong Kong Dollar	HKD	Uganda	New Shilling	UGS
Hungary	Forint	HUF	United Arab Emirates	Dirham	AED
Iceland	Krone	ISK			
India	Indian Rupee	INR	United Kingdom	Sterling	GBP
Indonesia	Rupiah	IDR	United States	United States Dollar	USD
Iran	Rial	IRR	Vanuatu	Vatu	VUV
Ireland	Irish Punt	IEP	Zaire Republic	Zaire	CFA
Israel	Shekel	ISS	Zambia	Kwacha	ZMK
Italy	Lira	ITL	Zimbabwe	Zimbabwe Dollar	ZWD
Ivory Coast	CFA Franc	XOF			

Strong treasury controls are essential to the management of foreign exchange exposure.

The control framework

- A statement of treasury objectives and policies
- The procedures manual
- Key control mechanisms
- Sources of advice
- Disclosure statements
- The role of the external auditors
- Ethical issues

As we have discussed throughout this book, the management of the currency risks that are created by an organization's trading activities is a key role of the treasury function. In performing this role, however, the treasury will create new risks that are potentially as damaging to the organization as the underlying trading risks. Among these treasury management risks are those of financial loss arising from fraud, speculation, counterparty failure and incompetence. While most of the treasury disasters that have occurred in both corporates and financial institutions in recent years can be attributed to one of these causes, the fundamental problem in each case was not so much that the disaster occurred but that the control framework was inadequate to prevent it.

Strong and effective treasury controls are absolutely essential to the responsible management of foreign exchange exposure, and those who bear such responsibility (from board level downwards) have no excuse if a disaster occurs because of a weakness in controls. There is no shortage of advice available, or of object lessons from others' experience, to guide those wishing to do everything possible to create a secure environment within which treasury activities can be carried out. In this chapter we will discuss the need for treasury controls, the control mechanisms that should be present and the guidelines issued by interested organizations for the benefit of those dealing in the foreign exchange markets.

Why do we need treasury controls?

The treasury is perhaps the one function within an organization that has the ability to destroy that organization's financial position overnight. Tremendous power is commonly given to relatively junior treasury staff to commit the organization to major financial transactions and to transfer significant amounts out of the company's bank accounts in settlement of those transactions. It is frequently the case that a company may require the signatures of two directors on a cheque for £5 000 but, at the same time, allow a treasury dealer to buy $50 million and debit the bank account to pay for them without reference to anyone else.

An organization's treasury risks can be categorized as:

- operational risks (such as currency exposures) that derive from its trading activities, for which *management* controls are required, and

- risks arising from the way in which the treasury performs its functions, for which *organizational* controls are required.

Operational risks are controlled by having efficient, accurate and timely processes for reporting and forecasting currency positions and exposures to the treasury so that they can be managed in accordance with approved policies and strategies. Organizational controls ensure that the processes of dealing and settlement are managed and monitored to prevent losses arising from fraud, error, speculation and counterparty failure. We have discussed the need for, and the approach to, exposure forecasting and reporting in earlier chapters. In this chapter we will therefore focus on organizational controls.

The key treasury control mechanisms are:

- a statement of treasury objectives and policies
- a comprehensive procedures manual, and
- a system of controls that ensures that the policies and procedures are implemented within a secure environment.

A statement of treasury objectives and policies

As we discussed in Chapter 3, the foundation for the control of treasury is a board-approved written statement of treasury objectives and policies based on the company's risk management philosophy. The outline of a policy statement is set out in Chapter 3, together with examples of the kinds of policies that are typically established for service centre treasuries.

Once the objectives and policies have been formulated, documented and approved, it is necessary to produce a procedures manual which describes how the treasury will put the policies into effect on a day-to-day basis and the control framework within which these processes take place. Both the policy and procedures documents should be reviewed regularly (for example, at annual interviews) and there should be an approved process for authorizing any changes to their provisions.

The procedures manual

The documented procedures for foreign exchange exposure management should cover the following activities:

Identification of exposure This should include a brief definition of the different types of exposure incurred by the company, the forecasting and reporting processes and responsibilities within the group and, if used, the procedure for identifying the net group exposure.

Types of permitted hedging instrument The permitted hedging instruments (for example, spot, forward, option-dated, and purchased currency option) should be briefly described and the criteria for the selection of a particular hedging instrument to be used in a given exposure situation should be explained.

Selection of counterparties The basis on which counterparties are selected for individual transactions should be set out. This might cover the number of counterparties required for deals of different sizes; for example, one counterparty for a deal below £50 000 or equivalent, two counterparties up to, say, £10 million, and three counterparties for deals in excess of £10 million.

The counterparties might be selected on the basis of past dealing performance, so that the bank that won the last deal in the same currency pair is automatically selected for the next deal, a second bank is chosen on its performance over the previous six months, and a third bank might be selected on a rota basis from other banks that make a book in one or other of the currencies of the transaction. The analysis of banks' dealing performance will come either from the database within the treasury computer system or from manually maintained records. The procedures manual should explain the process for recording such information.

There will also be control factors that will influence the choice of counterparties to be used for particular deals. Clearly, the deal must not result in a breach of the limit set for any counterparty. There must also be a current mandate in place and this mandate should have been formally accepted by the counterparty. The company may also stipulate that the counterparty must have been set up on its computer system so that the deal can be processed.

Market rate informaiton Market rate information can come from a variety of sources, including an on-line electronic system, banks and brokers, and financial publications. It may be used in developing hedging strategies or for choosing the optimum time at which to hedge. The manual should describe both the sources of rate information available to the treasury and the purposes for which it will be used.

If deals have to be authorized in advance by various levels of senior management depending upon the size, the maturity period or the instrument used for the transaction, the authority levels should be set out in the procedures manual together with details of how the authorization is to be documented; for example, by a signature on the deal ticket.

Deal authorization procedures

The manual should set out basic guidelines as to how dealing should be conducted. Such guidelines might read as follows:

Dealing procedure

- The appropriate number of banks must be selected according to the size of the deal and previous dealing performance, as set out in the procedures for selection of counterparties.

- Each treasury dealer will be provided with a partially completed deal ticket and will contact one of the selected banks.

> *Market rate information can come from a variety of sources.*

- The deal details must be advised to all of the banks simultaneously.

- Any bank that fails to answer the telephone within ten seconds will be eliminated and may be replaced with a substitute bank.

- Any quote that differs materially from the current Reuters' rate, or the expected rate, or a competing bank's rate must be queried immediately.

- The bank quoting the best rate wins the deal.

- If the quotes received are the same, the bank quoting first wins the deal.

- One dealer must close the deal with the winning bank before the other bank(s) are told that they have lost.

- The current Reuters' rate and the time must be noted on the deal ticket at the time of dealing.

- The dealer must repeat the details of the deal clearly to the winning bank after the deal has been struck. (As has been noted in Chapter 7, it is standard practice for banks to tape record all dealing conversations so that a record of what was said can be referred to in the event of a dispute. In view of this, it is desirable that the company's dealers speak clearly, concisely and unambiguously to avoid the risk of misinterpretation.)

Documentation The documentation of foreign exchange transactions is a key part of the treasury control process and, of course, also generates the information that enters the accounting and management reporting systems. The procedures manual should describe in detail the documentation requirements and provide examples of relevant documents.

The main documents used for controlling corporate treasury dealing activities are:

● deal requests from subsidiaries (where relevant)

● deal tickets (a specimen deal ticket is to be found in Appendix 1 at the end of this chapter)

● outgoing confirmation letters (a specimen confirmation is to be found in Appendix 2)

● incoming confirmation letters from counterparties

● settlement instructions, where settlement is not initiated electronically.

Deal settlement The procedures for the settlement of transactions must be tightly controlled as any weaknesses can provide opportunities to defraud the company. It should be remembered that a maturing foreign exchange transaction will involve two flows of money, a payment of funds from the company to the bank counterparty and a receipt of funds by the company from the counterparty. The settlement procedures must ensure that there is no opportunity for funds to be fraudulently debited from the company's bank accounts, or diverted after a legitimate debit instruction has been given. Equally, the company must ensure that all proceeds that are due to be received by it as a result of foreign exchange transactions are delivered to its bank accounts and are not able to be diverted elsewhere. The key control mechanisms for providing the required security are bank mandates, funds transfer authorities and restrictions on beneficiaries, and segregation of duties. These are described in detail later in this chapter.

> *The documentation of foreign exchange transactions is a key part of the treasury control process.*

Accounting There are a variety of ways in which accounting information relating to treasury transactions is produced by corporates. This ranges from manual book-keeping by the treasury dealer at one extreme to an electronic feed from the treasury computer system into the accounting system at the other extreme. The procedures manual should document the responsibilities, information, formats, and timings as well as the methods by which accounting entries are to be generated.

Management reporting is an important but frequently inadequate, part **Management** of the control process. In its widest sense, management reporting for **reporting** control purposes should include information that enables strategic risk management decisions to be made as well as providing confirmation that policies and controls have been complied with. Management reporting and performance measurement are discussed in more detail in Chapter 9.

The average corporate treasury uses a number of electronic systems, **Systems** from balance and transaction reporting to a treasury workstation. The procedures manual should describe all of the systems used and their purposes and provide detailed operating instructions noting, where relevant, the controls over access to, or use of, particular systems. It is essential, when describing treasury systems, to state clearly the use to which information obtained from such systems is put as well as to explain how such information is obtained.

> *Management reporting is an important part of the control process.*

Disaster recovery is an issue which has become more prominent in recent **Disaster** years with the disruption to business life from terrorist activity and com- **prevention and** puter hackers and viruses. As a result, disaster prevention and recovery **recovery** are now common features of treasury procedures manuals. The objective of the recovery plan is to enable the work of the treasury to continue with the minimum of disruption after a disaster.

The types of action typically covered in disaster prevention and recovery plans include:

- procedures to save computer data and store it offsite on a daily Disaster prevention basis
- procedures to protect against, and detect, any attempt at unauthorized access
- procedures to protect against computer viruses, for example by controlling the source of software, and
- the use of an uninterruptible power supply for the computer systems which allows information to be stored and the systems to be shutdown in an orderly manner without loss of data in the event of a power cut.

Disaster recovery Disaster recovery procedures are often based on having back-up facilities at a remote site (not elsewhere on the same site) to which the treasury can move at a moment's notice and, with the use of the stored computer data, resume operations without undue delay. Effective disaster recovery procedures should cover a range of potential situations from the comparatively minor power cut, through being denied access to the building in which the treasury is located, to the complete destruction of the building.

It is worth bearing in mind when formulating disaster recovery plans that the work of the treasury could be disrupted by a disaster at one of its bank counterparties. Disaster planning should therefore take into consideration the ways in which the company can ensure that it is not prevented from carrying out its functions by a problem at one of its banks. One simple way to deal with this is to ensure that the company has a number of counterparty banks and that it has agreed a course of action with each bank to be taken in the event of a disaster.

Organizational matters The procedures manual should include an explanation of how the treasury relates to other financial departments and fits into the overall management structure of the company. This is most easily achieved by the inclusion of organization charts, with some explanatory text. Other valuable organizational information that should be included are job descriptions of each member of the treasury team. The production of a job description is often useful in assisting personnel to focus on their role and responsibilities and to identify key and subsidiary tasks. One of the benefits of producing formal job descriptions is that greater efficiency is achieved as work is more focused on priority issues and those areas in which work is either duplicated or not performed are identified and eliminated. An additional benefit is that controls can be enhanced by making it clear in a job description where the segregation of duties occurs.

Key control mechanisms

Dealing mandates The dealing mandate is the prime control over the company's relationship with the banks that it uses for hedging foreign exchange exposure. The main purpose of the mandate is to authorize the bank to act on instructions to enter into foreign exchange contracts and accept payment instructions from named officers of the company so that hedging actions can be implemented and settled. From the company's point of view, however, it is essential that the banks are authorized to accept only those instructions that are in conformity with approved policies and controls. The mandate therefore has an additional role as a control mechanism. In this role it can be used to ensure that dealing is carried out within defined parameters, to assist the monitoring of transactions and to control the movement of funds.

The key features of the dealing mandate typically include:

- the names of the people who are authorized to give instructions to the bank to enter into foreign exchange hedging transactions
- the name(s) of the entities on whose behalf they are authorized to deal (this might, for example, include the central treasury vehicle and subsidiary companies)
- the types of instrument that the dealers are authorized to use. This is likely to include spot, forward, swap and option dated forward contracts. It may also include currency options, but with the stipulation that the company's dealers can only enter into contracts to *purchase* options and not to *write* (sell) them
- limits on the maximum amounts, currencies or maturity period of transactions. This enables the company to prevent its dealers from arranging large value contracts in exotic currencies maturing at a distant future date when such contracts are not required
- the names of the people who are authorized to sign deal confirmation letters together with specimen signatures (for an effective segregation of duties, these should not include people who are authorized to deal)
- the names of the people authorized to give instructions for the payment of currency purchased together with specimen signatures (these may be the same people as those authorized to sign deal confirmations). Payment of currency purchased will either be direct to a third party, in which case it is essential to have strict controls in place, or to a bank account held in the name of the company. Many companies follow the practice of taking the proceeds of all foreign exchange transactions into their own bank accounts and paying funds away to third parties as necessary from those accounts using the normal bank account signatory controls. Where all funds are initially received into

one of the company's bank accounts, this should be incorporated as a standing instruction in the mandate and a list of the accounts attached as an appendix.

- a statement to the effect that the company will confirm every transaction in writing within a specified time period (for example, to be received by the bank within three working days) and a requirement for the bank to contact a named individual (not a treasury dealer) if the confirmation has not been received within that time

- a requirement for the bank to confirm every transaction in writing within a specified time period to a named individual (ideally outside the treasury)

- a request for a named and authorized officer of the bank to accept the mandate formally by signing and returning a copy of it to a named individual. The accepted copy of the mandate is often sent to a senior manager outside of the treasury department, such as the company secretary. Formal acceptance of the mandate provides confirmation that the bank has actually received the mandate and implies that it understands the terms on which the company is prepared to transact foreign exchange business with it.

A dealing mandate is a very powerful tool and it should be subject to tight controls by the company. It should be issued by someone of appropriate seniority who has been authorized by the board to do so. Each page of the mandate should be numbered and signed by the authorized issuer(s) to prevent a mandate which bears genuine signatures on its final page being altered for fraudulent purposes. Access to copies of the mandate should also be tightly controlled; it is not unknown for unauthorized personnel, such as cleaners, to misuse mandates that they have found lying on desks or in easily accessible files. Mandates should be updated immediately if there is a change in the personnel authorized to give instructions to the banks.

A specimen dealing mandate is to be found in Appendix 3 at the end of this chapter.

Counterparty limits

Counterparty limits are used to control an organization's exposure to the risk of loss from counterparty failure. As far as foreign exchange is concerned the loss from the failure of a counterparty could be in terms of:

- the loss of the rate at which an organization has hedged itself (rate risk). If it is obliged to replace the cover by a new transaction with a different bank, this may have to be done at a worse rate (it should be remembered, however, that the loss of a rate may allow the organization to hedge at a better rate than the original one if the market has moved in its favour)

- the loss of principal if the counterparty defaults on settlement and currency that has been paid for is not delivered (settlement risk).

In managing counterparty risk, an organization should be concerned to ensure that it only deals with counterparties that meet specific standards of creditworthiness and that limits are placed on the amount of exposure to any one counterparty. The typical approach to satisfying these two needs is to deal only with banks that have a specified credit rating and to establish monetary limits for the maximum exposure to each bank.

A dealing mandate is a very powerful tool.

There are a number of rating agencies that assess creditworthiness and publish ratings for banks and other institutions. Among the better known, and most frequently used, are Standard and Poor's, Moody's, IBCA and Thomson BankWatch. The basic objective of the rating agencies is to evaluate the ability of banks and corporations to meet the timely payment of principal and interest on debt obligations. Ratings are split between short term (up to one year) and long term (over one year) and graded according to the agencies' opinion, after detailed analysis of a wide variety of information, as to the level of risk. Each grading is described in terms of the degree of risk expected.

An organization should determine what minimum credit rating it is prepared to accept for its counterparties and establish this as one criterion for managing counterparty risk. The level of the minimum rating should, of course, be consistent with the organization's overall appetite for risk; if it is highly risk averse, it should require a high rating, if it has some appetite for risk it might set a lower minimum rating.

Having set a minimum credit rating for its counterparty banks it is necessary for the organization to establish procedures for monitoring that the counterparties continue to meet the rating and have not been downgraded. The rating agencies provide information to subscribers to assist this process. Most agencies publish monthly rating reports and will announce when a re-rating is likely.

The second element in the control of counterparty risk is to establish monetary limits for the absolute amount of exposure to be incurred to each bank. This is often a subjective process, based on perceptions of how competitive individual banks are. The tendency is to want to be able to transact as much business as possible with a competitive bank and therefore to give it a comparatively high limit. It should be remembered, however, that a competitive bank is not necessarily financially sound and that, although some protection may be gained from establishing a reasonably high credit rating criterion, this must be complemented by appropriate monetary limits. The overall objective in setting monetary limits should be to achieve a gross amount of limits spread across a range of banks so as to enable flexibility in dealing and a low level of exposure (for example, no more than ten per cent of outstanding hedges) to any individual bank.

It is common practice, when setting monetary limits, to apply the full value of a spot transaction but only a percentage of the value of forward contracts and currency options to the limit. The rationale for this reflects the difference in the financial impact between settlement risk, where the maximum loss is 100 per cent of the value of the transaction, and rate risk where any loss will be a lower percentage depending upon the degree to which adverse currency movements have taken place (and where there is potential for favourable movements).

Weightings for limit utilization purposes might, therefore, be set by the organization as follows:

Transaction type	Percentage of limit
Spot deal	100%
Forward contract	10%
Currency option	5% (per annum)

Thus an organization with £50 million worth of forward contracts outstanding with a particular bank would only charge 10 per cent of the value of these – £5 million – against the overall limit it had established for the bank. One difficulty that arises when a proportion of the value of a contract is charged to the limit is the treatment when a forward contract comes within two working days of its maturity date. Should it then be treated like a spot contract to reflect the fact that the full value of the transaction is now exposed to settlement risk? Logically it should, but in practice this is often found to create the difficulty that the limit is thereby breached. It is not uncommon to find that there is an inconsistency in the way that limit utilization is treated as organizations grapple with, or simply ignore, this problem and spot deals are treated differently from maturing forward contracts.

Two-way deal confirmation and confirmation reconciliation procedures **Confirmation** enable misunderstandings between the organization and the bank to be **and** identified and resolved and, more importantly from a control point of **reconciliation** view, are the means by which unrecorded deals and unauthorized dealing can be detected.

If misunderstandings, errors, unrecorded deals and unauthorized dealing are all to be detected, it is essential that *all* transactions, including spot deals, are confirmed and reconciled without fail. Any weaknesses in the system, or exceptions to the rules, open a loophole of risk through which, at worst, fraud or speculation could take place and, at best, simple errors could lead to additional time and expense being incurred to correct them.

> *Deal confirmation and reconciliation can be performed either manually or electronically.*

As a general principle, an organization should generate and issue its own confirmation letter, on the dealing date or as soon as possible thereafter, using information that is recorded in its systems and giving, where appropriate, payment instructions. The confirmation should be signed by authorized signatories named in the dealing mandate. It is not uncommon for banks to request their counterparties to confirm transactions by signing and returning a copy of the bank's own confirmation. This should be avoided both because the company's confirmation should not be dependent upon the receipt of a bank confirmation and because bank confirmations appear in a wide variety of formats and include differing, and sometimes inadequate, information.

Deal confirmation and reconciliation can be performed either manually or electronically. Whichever method is used, it is essential that the processes are performed by someone independent of the dealing function. Clearly, if a dealer is allowed to check incoming confirmations, or is able to intercept before someone else reconciles them, it would be possible for him to conceal an unauthorized transaction. Many companies avoid the risk of dealer interception or of two treasury staff working in collusion to conceal transactions by placing responsibility for confirmation reconciliation outside of the treasury.

The benefits of confirmation reconciliation as a control mechanism will be greatly diminished, however, if incoming confirmations are not received promptly. It is important, therefore, to have a procedure in place for logging the receipt of confirmations and chasing those that are outstanding after the time period laid down in the mandate. If late confirmations are not chased assiduously there is a risk that the banks will infer that it is not necessary to confirm transactions at all.

If a discrepancy is identified between the company's record of a transaction and the bank's record, it is necessary for there to be a procedure for investigating the discrepancy that does not give the dealer an opportunity to cover up a problem. The best approach, therefore, is for the person responsible for reconciling transactions to contact the bank direct and to resolve the matter either with the bank's back office or its dealer. Where there is a dispute, recourse is likely to be made to the tape recording of the dealing conversation to resolve the matter.

Segregation of duties

Segregation of duties has been referred to throughout this chapter and is a fundamental control mechanism. While it is impossible to prevent collusion among treasury staff to commit fraud or to speculate, collusion is both less likely to occur and, if it does occur, less likely to be successful if there is an effective segregation of duties. Segregation of duties does, of course, not only assist in the prevention of fraud and unauthorized dealing, it can also help in the identification of errors and in the monitoring of compliance with controls generally.

The objective of segregation is to prevent any one person from being able to perform all the functions necessary to deal, confirm, settle and report without being monitored by anyone else.

The processes which should be segregated, and the suggested job positions for each element of the work, are:

Activity	Job position
Deal authorization	Depending upon size/type of deal
Dealing	Dealer(s)
Deal recording	Back office administrator
Confirmation production	Back office administrator
Confirmation signing	Authorized signatories
Preparation of settlement instruction	Back office administrator
Signing of settlement instruction	Authorized signatories
Receipt/reconciliation of incoming confirmation	Non-treasury department, e.g. accounts department
Management reporting	Back office administrator/treasury analysts
Accounting	Back office administrator/treasury analysts

Ideally, the treasurer should not be authorized to deal if he or she is also authorized to sign deal and settlement confirmations.

A common practical problem with regard to the segregation of duties is that there are too few staff in the treasury to be able to achieve an effective segregation. In such cases, it is often necessary to involve personnel from other departments for key functions. Any organization that has limited staff available should, when reviewing the need for segregation, examine at which points it would be possible, in the absence of segregation, to commit a fraud or arrange unauthorized deals and then introduce segregation or additional checking at these points.

The objectives of management reporting, from a control point of view, are to provide senior management with the information necessary for them to ascertain that the treasury is complying with approved policies, strategies and controls. **Management reporting**

The requirements for control reports are therefore that they should be frequent (monthly rather than quarterly), show up-to-date information, and be focused on the key issues and measures. Management reporting generally covers a wide range of issues, depending upon the complexity of the treasury's activities (this is covered in more detail in Chapter 9). Controls reporting, which should normally be a section within the wider treasury reporting package, should be more succinct.

A control report might therefore include the following features:

- actual levels of hedging compared with required levels of hedging. For example, if the treasury is required to hedge a minimum of 60 per cent of forecast exposures for the period four to six months ahead, the report should demonstrate compliance with this;
- a report, which might be an exception report, confirming compliance with specific controls or noting and explaining breaches of them. This might, for example, cover confirmation of all deals by both sides, no discrepancies between the company's and the bank's records and compliance with counterparty limits.

Reporting of controls compliance is essential if controls are to be effective. Experience suggests that, where compliance with a control is not monitored, the control often ceases to be observed. Senior management would, furthermore, find it very embarrassing to have to admit after a treasury disaster that, although they had established a policy and control framework for the treasury, they had not actually bothered to check that it was being complied with.

Internal audit The internal audit function is often asked to review the treasury department but, equally often, has only a limited understanding of treasury activities and the instruments used for hedging. An internal audit of treasury tends, therefore, to focus on checking the completeness of documentation and reconciliation with bank statements. This is useful for confirming low level compliance with controls but is unlikely to identify more fundamental issues relating to compliance with policies, opportunities to improve efficiency, the accuracy of risk identification, and so on.

> *Reporting of controls compliance is essential if controls are to be effective.*

An internal audit can provide optimum value when it is performed by staff with a broad understanding of treasury objectives, techniques, strategies and controls. Such experience can often be provided by using staff who have spent time in the treasury department or who have gained experience of treasury in other organizations. Where such expertise is not available, companies often use external consultants to audit the treasury.

An internal audit of a treasury's foreign exchange exposure management activities should cover the following matters:

- the continuing relevance of the policies in view of any changes there may have been in the company's operations or the foreign exchange markets; for example, the introduction of new hedging instruments

- any consequential changes that may be needed, as a result of amended policies, to the documentation of procedures or the control environment

- the accuracy of risk identification and the efficiency of risk reporting processes within the company

- the effectiveness of the control procedures as they are implemented on a day-to-day basis

- treasury systems and their security

- the understanding in other departments, divisions and subsidiaries that interface with the treasury of the treasury objectives, policies and controls

- the content, format and quality of management reporting, and

- the reliability of the accounting for foreign exchange transactions and positions.

Sources of advice

A number of bodies that are actively involved in the financial markets have issued useful advice on the control of foreign exchange dealing. The aspects that are of particular relevance to organizations in the corporate sector are summarized below.

The Association of Corporate Treasurers in the United Kingdom has published *Good Practice Guidance on Foreign Exchange and Money Market Dealing Procedures and the Exchange of Confirmations*. The guidance note has been produced by the ACT's Technical Committee to enable treasurers to deal with important practical problems and to benefit from the experience of other members of the Association.

The Association of Corporate Treasurers' Guidelines

The process by which guidelines are produced is typically as follows. The guideline is initiated by an approach from a member of the Association seeking advice on a particular problem. The Technical Committee undertakes in-depth research into the matter and in the course of this will usually discuss with members in a range of industries and in other professional bodies, such as the British Bankers Association. The result of this research is a guidance note in the form of an exposure draft which is published in *The Treasurer*, the official publication of the ACT. During the exposure period, the Technical Committee considers any comments that it receives on the exposure draft and these may be incorporated in the final guidance note.

The ACT stresses that the guidance note is intended to illustrate the key control features that should be in place and is not intended to be a substitute for the policy and procedures manual that should be prepared and implemented in every treasury operation.

The guidance note recommends that the following controls, which are discussed in detail earlier in this chapter, should be in place:

- segregation of duties between dealing, deal processing, settlement and reconciliation
- dealing mandates that reinforce the controls over individual's dealing authorities and the segregation of duties with regard to the reconciliation of confirmations

- counterparty limits and the monitoring of limit utilization
- simultaneous competitive quoting
- tape recording of dealing and settlement telephones
- the use of sequentially numbered deal tickets, or substitute controls in 'paperless' dealing rooms
- full recording of every deal
- two-way confirmation of all deals
- chasing procedures for late confirmations and speedy resolution of any discrepancies between the company's records and the banks' confirmations.

The London Code of Conduct

The *London Code of Conduct*, issued by the Bank of England, sets out the principles and standards which broking firms, financial institutions and other providers of financial services (and their employees) who are supervised under the Financial Services Act 1986 are expected to observe in the wholesale markets. While these standards are only mandatory for those corporate treasuries that are designated as permitted persons under the Act, they do provide best practice guidelines that all treasuries would do well to follow.

The code is divided into a number of sections; the key points of which for those managing currency exposure include:

Responsibilities

- The responsibility to ensure that any individual who commits the firm to a transaction has the necessary authority to do so. This should be addressed by the company establishing internal authority limits and through the terms of its dealing mandates.

- The necessity for those operating in the market (principally dealers but including those who instruct or supervise dealers) to be adequately trained in the practices of the market and to know their own and their firm's responsibilities. The training of employees is the responsibility of the principal.

- Dealers must not misrepresent the nature of a transaction and must be clear as to what instruments have been dealt. Dealing must therefore take place in a transparent manner.

- Principals and brokers are required to know their customer and to be able to establish, before dealing, that the customer understands the instrument being discussed, particularly if it is a derivative instrument. From a corporate's point of view, this point underlines the importance of establishing good banking relationships and authorizing dealing only in appropriate and clearly understood instruments.

- Both parties must understand the basis on which a quote is made, and in particular whether it is firm or merely indicative. Both parties 'should regard themselves as bound to a deal once the price and any other key commercial terms have been agreed'.

- The Code gives guidance on the requirements for tape recording deals as a means by which disputes can be quickly resolved.

Dealing principles and procedures

- The Code advises that 'prompt passing, recording and careful checking of confirmations is vital to minimize the possibility of areas of misunderstanding whether dealing direct or through brokers' and goes on to state that 'in all markets, the confirmation (whether posted, telexed or sent by other electronic means) provides a necessary final safeguard against dealing errors. Confirmations should be dispatched and checked carefully and promptly even when oral checks have been undertaken. The issue and checking of confirmations is a back office responsibility which should be carried out independently from those who initiate deals'.

Settlement and confirmations

> *The standards of control expected by the Bank of England from financial institutions are applicable to other organizations.*

Clearly, the standards of control that the Bank of England expects from financial institutions are applicable to other organizations and should, where relevant and practically possible, be implemented by them.

The G30, an organization of senior bankers and other market participants, issued a report in July 1992 on the use of derivatives and appropriate control procedures. The report is intended primarily for market professionals (such as banks) and is less concerned with the requirements of end users (such as corporates). Many of its comments and recommendations are therefore not relevant to the typical corporate user of derivatives and these have been excluded from the summary below. The key recommendations in the G30 report that are relevant to corporate users of derivatives are:

The G30 (Group of Thirty) Report

- Senior management and board members should have sufficient understanding of derivatives to be able to approve policies relating to risk appetite and strategy. These policies need to be clearly defined, communicated, and implemented by management at all levels.

- Dealers should mark their positions to market on at least a daily basis. (Corporates may feel that weekly or monthly is more appropriate.)

- Users of derivatives should use Value at Risk analysis to provide a benchmark to measure market risk. This should measure the effect on net worth at both a given confidence level and over a particular time horizon, based on past experience of movements in underlying prices, volatility, and so on.

- Dealers should forecast cash and borrowing requirements (or currency cash flows).

- To the extent that it is appropriate, end users should adopt the same risk management procedures as market professionals.

- Exposures on all products should be aggregated by counterparty to determine the overall exposure to each counterparty.

- Both dealing and back office staff should have sufficient experience and skill in derivatives. Contingency plans should be in place to cater for the loss of key members of staff.

- Users should have adequate systems for data capture, risk management, settlement and management reporting.

- Management should authorize specific people to commit the organization to derivatives' transactions and ensure that counterparty banks are aware of who they are. This should be effected by means of dealing mandates.

- The financial statements should contain sufficient information to explain why derivatives' transactions were undertaken, the degree of risk involved and how they are accounted for.

The Futures and Options Association

The Futures and Options Association is a trade association based in London for companies, firms and other organizations which transact business in futures, options or derivatives or which use these instruments in the course of their business activities. The FOA has a membership internationally of some 200 banks, other financial institutions, commodity houses, brokers, fund managers, exchanges, lawyers and accountants. The role of the FOA is to represent the derivatives' industry and to protect the interests of its membership.

In December 1995, the FOA issued a document entitled 'Managing Derivatives Risk, Guidelines for End-users of Derivatives'. This publication was specifically produced for the benefit of users and potential users of derivatives who are end-users rather than brokers or dealers. The committee that drew up the guidelines was drawn from a range of organizations including banks, insurance companies, fund managers, pension funds, corporate treasury, lawyers and accountants.

The FOA's guidelines focus on what it sees as six core principles for managing derivatives' risk. These principles are intended to apply as widely as possible and are aimed both at organizations using derivatives for their own account as well as those acting on behalf of customers. The principles (which, incidentally, largely echo those proposed by other organizations) can be summarized as follows:

- The board of directors (or its equivalent) should establish and approve effective policies for the use of derivatives including, specifically, the instruments to be used and how they are to be used. These should be consistent with the organization's commercial strategy and risk appetite.

- Senior management should establish clear written procedures for implementing the policy. These should include such issues as authorities, reporting, limits, counterparty and documentation approval and valuation procedures.

- There should be an effective framework of internal controls and audits to ensure compliance with both external regulations and internal policies.

- There should be a sound risk management function that provides an independent framework for all aspects of reporting, monitoring and control of the risk management process.

- Procedures should be established to enable the organization to perform a full analysis of all credit risks and to be able to minimize those risks.

- Procedures should also be set up for monitoring and managing legal risk. These should cover matters of legal capacity and authority, compliance with statutory requirements and documentation regarding the dealing relationship and the terms of transactions.

The Guidelines define the above issues clearly and explain in detail how the FOA advises that organizations should implement the six principles. Copies of the document are available from the FOA at its offices at Roman Wall House, 1–2 Crutched Friars, London EC3N 2AN, UK.

The Accounting Standards Board The ASB statement issued in July 1993 on the elements to be reported in the *Operating and Financial Review* (OFR) section of the annual report provides the basis for a discussion of treasury policies and controls. The recommended disclosure is regarded as essentially voluntary and is intended as an amplification of the information that is provided in the company's 'Cadbury' disclosure statement. The key elements relating to foreign exchange management that might be reported are:

- treasury policies and objectives, including the management of currency risk, borrowing currencies, use of financial instruments for hedging, and the extent to which net currency investments are hedged by currency borrowings and other hedging instruments, and

- exchange controls and other restrictions on the ability to transfer funds.

Disclosure statements

It is becoming increasingly common for companies to make disclosure statements in their annual report about treasury management. These statements perform a number of functions. Their primary purposes are to inform shareholders of the approach to managing key risks and to confirm that the board is aware of, and has approved, the policies. The disclosure statement should indicate that the policies have been formulated in a logical and structured way and are appropriate to the risks being managed. Finally, disclosure should also confirm that there are effective procedures in place by which the policies are implemented and that the control and reporting framework has also been established. The disclosure statement should therefore provide a basis for shareholders (particularly institutional ones) to ask relevant questions about the implementation of the policies.

The Association of Corporate Treasurers has issued a statement on treasury disclosure. Its stated purpose is to 'provide a coherent guideline to good practice when information about treasury risks and their management is being communicated to shareholders or other interested parties outside the company'.

For each main area of treasury activity, including foreign exchange management, the Association considers that the following information is relevant to investors and should be considered for disclosure:

- a brief description of the key issues and exposures

- a reference to the process for identifying and measuring the exposure

- a comment on the significance of the risk to the current and future performance of the business

- a statement of the company's policy in managing the risk, to include the rationale for the policy, the proportions and time horizon of hedging, the scope for discretion, the instruments used for hedging and any risk arising from the use of the instruments

- a confirmation that the policy is complied with, and an explanation of any circumstances where this may not be the case, and

- a statement on the organization and control of treasury activities.

It will be noted that for the directors to make such disclosures in good faith it is necessary for them to be provided with the information on which to base such statements. Management reporting, as discussed in Chapter 9, should *inter alia* provide the information to support the disclosure statements.

The Association of Corporate Treasurers has issued a statement on treasury disclosure.

With regard to foreign exchange management the ACT specifically recommends that disclosure should cover the following matters.

- A brief description of the Group's exposure to significant transaction and balance sheet risks, both direct and indirect and short and long term.

    An understanding of the strategic risks stemming from the operational currencies of markets, competitors and production is particularly important. Terms used to define risk should be defined to avoid misinterpretation.

- Policy for the management of each type of risk, including reference to the degree of discretion exercised in covering commercial risk and establishing uncovered currency positions.

- Material foreign exchange gains and losses associated with liquidity management and material cashflow effects of balance sheet hedges.

The ACT also recommends that disclosure should explain how currency risks are managed. This should include 'the manner in which the Board controls treasury management and hedging activity. This will usually include the level of decentralization, the delegation of authority, the degree to which a view (on future movements in market rates) may be exercised, the hedging methods which may be used and the nature and frequency of reporting to the Board'.

The role of the external auditors

The external auditors are required to form an opinion on the accounts. In doing so, they will audit the foreign exchange transactions and examine bank statements, confirmation letters and any other documentation relating to those transactions. While this can enable them to identify what deals have been done, what flows of currency have occurred and the positions held on the bank accounts, it will not necessarily tell them whether currency risk is being properly identified and managed or whether the control environment is adequate. Specialized treasury expertise is required to answer these more fundamental questions.

The major audit firms typically have management consultancy practices that include treasury consultants. These consultants may participate in audits to provide specialist treasury advice on policies, procedures and controls within the clients' treasuries to the audit team. Treasury consultants also, of course, provide advice on other aspects of foreign exchange exposure management and will normally form a view on the overall appropriateness and effectiveness of the risk management processes during the course of an audit and bring any areas of concern to the attention of the company. The use of the resources of the external auditors to perform a focused health check can therefore be a quick and cost-effective way of ensuring that currency exposure management is efficient or of identifying weaknesses that should be remedied.

Ethical issues

Treasury staff are frequently offered hospitality, gifts or other services by financial institutions with whom they come into contact in the course of their work. This can give rise to ethical dilemmas and in these circumstances there is a need for an organization to establish clear principles and rules. These rules should prohibit treasury personnel from accepting any benefit that could affect, or appear to affect, their judgement, loyalty or the proper performance of their duties, particularly where this might result in business being channelled to a particular counterparty to the detriment of the company.

Additionally, the rules should require that the employer should be informed if treasury personnel conduct personal business with institutions that also seek to do business with it, and any personal benefits that may accrue to the employee as a result of such personal business.

Summary

Adequate and effectively implemented controls are essential to the responsible management of foreign exchange exposure. Treasury risks arise both from an organization's trading activities and from its treasury operations and the control framework should cover both of these areas.

The treasury should have a procedures manual that documents the processes by which foreign exchange exposure is managed and the control mechanisms that are in place. The key control elements are:

- dealing and transfer mandates
- counterparty limits
- two-way deal confirmation
- confirmation reconciliation
- segregation of duties
- management reporting, including reporting on controls compliance, and
- internal audit.

A number of professional bodies have issued advice on treasury controls. Organizations that deal in foreign exchange should ensure that their dealing operations conform with recognized best practice.

Appendix 1

(Company name) plc
FOREIGN EXCHANGE DEAL TICKET

CONTRACT NO.   DEALING DATE:

SPOT/FORWARD DEAL   DEAL AUTHORISED BY:

BUY/SELL	CURRENCY AMOUNT	AGAINST (CURRENCY)	VALUE DATE

BANK NAME	RATE	AMOUNT OF CONTRACURRENCY
(Bank 1)		
(Bank 2)		

REASON FOR DEAL

SETTLEMENT

CURRENCY BOUGHT DELIVER TO: (Bank name and address)

FOR ACCOUNT: (Account name and number)

CURRENCY SOLD DELIVER TO: (Bank name and address)

FOR ACCOUNT: (Account name and number)

AUTHORITIES

DEAL CONFIRMATION CHECKED AND SIGNED BY: DEALER ....

SIGNATORY 1 ....

SIGNATORY 2 ....

STERLING SETTLEMENT   Initials

INPUT TO CHAPS/EFT

CHAPS/EFT INPUT VERIFIED

CHAPS/EFT PAYMENT RELEASED

Appendix 2

(Company name) plc

To: *(Counterparty name)*
          (Address)

Contract No.

Date:

CONFIRMATION OF FOREIGN EXCHANGE CONTRACT

This is to confirm our foreign exchange contract arranged today on behalf of [name of company/subsidiary].

We buy   *(Currency and amount)*

Exchange rate

We sell   *(Currency and amount)*

Value date

SETTLEMENT

Please pay our currency purchased to: *(Bank name and address)*

For account: *(Account name and number)*

We deliver currency sold to your account at: *(Bank name and address)*

For account   *(Account name and number)*

Signed .... (Authorized signatory)

         .... (Authorized signatory)

Confirmation checked by dealer:

Appendix 3

(Company name) plc

To: (*Counterparty name*)
(*Address*)

Date:

Dear   ,

TREASURY DEALING MANDATE

This letter authorizes officers of [name of bank] to act on instructions from specified employees of [company name] in accordance with the conditions set out below. All previous treasury dealing mandates, instructions or authorities are hereby cancelled.

1 ARRANGEMENT OF FOREIGN EXCHANGE FACILITIES

The following personnel are authorized to arrange foreign exchange facilities on behalf of the company and its wholly-owned subsidiaries.

Finance Director
Group Treasurer

2 FOREIGN EXCHANGE TRANSACTIONS

2.1 Authorized instruments

The personnel listed in Section 2.2 below are authorized to arrange transactions by telephone in the following instruments on behalf, and in the name, of the company and its wholly-owned subsidiaries:

- short-term deposits with maturities not exceeding [three months] in foreign currencies

- call deposits in foreign currencies

- spot and forward foreign exchange contracts with maturities not exceeding [12 months]

- the purchase of currency options.

Page 1 of 2

2.2 Personnel authorized to arrange transactions

The personnel listed below are authorized to arrange the transactions specified in Section 2.1 above:

> Group Treasurer
> Assistant Treasurer
> Treasury Dealer

3 DEAL CONFIRMATIONS

It is company policy both to confirm all transactions in writing and to require counterparty banks to confirm transactions in writing. You are requested to send confirmation of each transaction within three working days to:

> Mr J Smith
> Group Financial Controller
> (*Company name*)
> (*Company address*)

You are also requested to inform Mr J Smith if you have not received a written confirmation of a transaction from the company within five working days of the dealing date.

4 SETTLEMENT

Maturing deposits and interest thereon, and the proceeds of foreign exchange transactions, must be paid to an account held in the name of the company or one of its subsidiaries as listed in Appendix 1 of this mandate.

5 AUTHORIZED SIGNATORIES

Written confirmations of deposit and foreign exchange transactions sent to you by the company must bear the original signatures of two authorized signatories as shown in Appendix 2 of this mandate. You are requested to contact Mr J Smith if you receive a confirmation which does not comply with this requirement.

6 ACCEPTANCE

You are requested to return the enclosed copy of this mandate signed by a named authorized officer of the bank and bearing the bank's seal or stamp to confirm acceptance of this mandate.

Signed .... (Authorized signatory)

.... (Authorized signatory)

Management reporting and performance measurement should enable the board and senior management to ascertain that the approved exposure management process is being followed.

Management reporting and performance measurement

9

- Risk assessment and management
- Performance measurement
- Performance measures
- Provision of other management information
- Monitoring compliance with controls
- Frequency of reporting
- Difficulties with performance measurement

As we have discussed earlier in this book, the analysis and reporting of foreign exchange exposures and hedging actions is a key part of the currency exposure management process. That process, as we have seen, includes the identification of exposures, the evaluation of the potential effects on profit of not hedging the exposure, the formulation of policies and procedures, the implementation of hedging strategies and compliance with the control mechanisms that ensure that the whole process is carried out within a secure environment.

Management reporting and performance measurement should provide the information, on a continuing basis, that enables the board and senior management to ascertain that the approved exposure management process is being followed and either that it is producing the desired results or, on the other hand, that it is not appropriate and should be changed. Such changes may be necessary for a variety of reasons; the volume and nature of exposures may change over time as the business develops and expands into new markets; the board may grow more familiar with the nature of the risks and wish to adopt a less cautious approach; or new risk management techniques and instruments may be introduced that allow a more proactive approach to be taken. Regular analysis and reporting of exposures and the effects of the organization's hedging strategies are essential if an objective appraisal of the risk management approach is to be made and opportunities to improve it are to be identified.

In this chapter we will consider the requirements for management reporting under four broad headings:

- for the purposes of risk assessment and management
- to measure the financial effects of the hedging strategy and to assess treasury efficiency – 'performance measurement'
- to provide information, and
- to monitor compliance with controls.

Risk assessment and management

As we saw in Chapter 2, the information requirements for a simple method of assessing currency risk are a forecast of net currency exposures, data relating to hedges that have been put in place, current spot and forward exchange rates and exchange rate forecasts. More complex measures of risk involving the use, for example, of the Monte Carlo and Value at Risk methodologies require different kinds of information, based either on historical market trends or on a large number of potential future exchange rate scenarios. These more complicated risk assessment techniques are widely used by financial institutions but at present are not commonly used by corporate treasuries. The main reasons for this are the differing objectives and time horizons of financial institutions and corporates. Corporate treasuries will generally aim to minimize exposures to risks that will arise as the result of trading activities during a future period while financial institutions make their money from the controlled creation and management of risk and are more concerned with how quickly they can close out a very short-term position if the market moves adversely.

Another reason that corporate treasuries tend to favour simple methods of risk assessment is that they are cheaper and easier to use and more readily understandable by senior management. Monte Carlo and Value at Risk techniques require complex data and sophisticated computer software, as well as computing time, whereas 'rule of thumb' measures can be calculated either manually or on a simple spreadsheet in a matter of moments to give a reasonable indication of the possible profit implications of the company's unhedged currency positions. A simple risk assessment report might appear as shown in the example below.

USD/GBP		Month 1	Month 2	Month 3
Net exposure (millions)		$(8.6)	$(7.5)	$(8.0)
Hedging actions		8.5	5.0	4.0
Unhedged position		$(0.1)	$(2.5)	$(4.0)
Percentage of exposure hedged		99%	67%	50%
	Spot			
Current market rates	$1.5300	$1.5360	$1.5210	$1.5175
GBP value at current rates (millions)		£(0.065)	£(1.644)	£(2.636)
Effect of 1 cent adverse movement (000)	£ –	£(11)	£(17)	
Effect of 5% adverse movement (000)	£(3)	£(86)	£(139)	
Forecast exchange rates		$1.5200	$1.5150	$1.5100
GBP value at forecast rates		£(0.065)	£(1.650)	£(2.649)
Forecast vs current rates (000)	£ –	£(6)	£(13)	

Example Currency risk assessment

Commentary

- The group has unhedged US Dollar exposures for the next three months totalling $6.6 million, equivalent to £4.3 million at current market rates.

- A 1 cent adverse movement in rates would cost the company £28 000.

- A 5 per cent adverse movement in rates would cost the company £228 000.

- The Dollar is expected to strengthen slightly over the next three months. A movement in line with current expectations would cost the company £19 000.

> *Corporate treasuries tend to favour simple methods of risk.*

The above report fulfils a number of functions. It shows the group's US Dollar/Sterling exposure before any hedging has been arranged, the hedging that is in place and the net unhedged position. It then indicates the Sterling cost of covering the remaining exposure at current market rates as well as providing various measures of the possible adverse effects of not hedging the outstanding exposure. Note also that the report includes a written, bullet point style, commentary. This is essential if the reader is to grasp quickly the key points that the report is intended to convey. Reports that are composed solely of columns of figures tend to confuse rather than inform their audience, particularly if they are provided to non-specialists.

These measures can be used as a quick indication of the currency risk that the company potentially faces. For example, if the effect of a 1 cent strengthening of the Dollar is to reduce profits by £28 000, a 4 cent movement would be (very roughly) worth £100 000. Similarly, if a 5 per cent movement in the Dollar costs the company £228 000, half a million pounds would be lost if it moved by 11 per cent. The company now has the basic information, taking into account also the forecast for exchange rates, that it requires to be able to determine whether it should increase its cover of its Dollar liabilities. It can therefore, formulate a currency management strategy on the basis of reasonably reliable information about its exposure to risk.

The important difference between this way of assessing risk and the Value at Risk methodology is that VaR aims to be able to indicate the *likelihood* of a particular risk outcome based on past experience of exchange rate movements. Value at Risk analysis, therefore, will express risk in the following way; 'it is 97.5 per cent (or some other selected percentage) certain that my loss will not be greater than £X thousand or million'. This does, of course, also mean that it is 2.5 per cent certain that a loss will exceed the same figure (and Value at Risk cannot tell you by how much it might exceed the stated amount).

The report also shows the percentage of cover taken against the net exposure. In our example, the level of cover for month 1 exposures is 99 per cent, for month 2 it is 67 per cent and for month 3 it is 50 per cent. Presentation of information in this way enables senior management (for example, the Treasury Committee) to monitor that policies or strategies that require specified maximum or minimum levels of cover are being complied with.

As we discussed at the beginning of this book, the assessment of currency risk is an essential step in establishing risk management policies and strategies. A report similar to the one shown on page 203, covering all the currencies in which a company has exposures, should be produced as a first step in the development of its risk management philosophy.

Performance measurement

Performance measurement, if it is to fulfil its purpose, must relate to the organization's currency exposure management objectives and policies. These, in turn, will determine the role of the treasury, in terms of its position on the cost centre/profit centre spectrum, and thus the approach that will be taken to hedge exposures.

As we noted in Chapter 3, there are a variety of ways in which treasury management can be approached – from the risk averse cost centre, through the value-added service centre, to the actively risk-seeking profit centre – and a number of ways in which exposure management can be organized. The measures used to assess the performance of the treasury must be relevant to the company's attitude to risk and the organizational arrangements and resources devoted to currency management. Beyond that, however, the company should not focus exclusively on the results of its hedging strategies, it should also attempt to measure the quality of

> *Performance measurement must relate to the organization's currency exposure management objectives and policies.*

its treasury function. To do both of these, it requires a mix of quantitative and qualitative benchmarks.

The risk averse *cost centre* treasury will typically be expected to hedge committed exposures fully as soon as they are identified and to cover forecast exposures in conformity with guidelines that specify particular minimum and maximum levels of cover to be taken depending upon how far forward the exposures are forecasted. There is, intentionally, little scope for the treasury to exercise judgement about how much cover to take or when to put it in place in a cost centre treasury; accordingly there is usually little emphasis on measuring the performance of the treasury in implementing these policies. The company's main concern is that the exposure is hedged; the rates at which the hedges have been arranged are usually regarded as being of lesser importance.

Performance measurement in a cost centre treasury, if it is carried out at all, is therefore likely to emphasize the qualitative aspects of its role as a provider of a service to group customers. If this is the case, however, and no attempt is made to assess the benefits of being risk averse the company will have failed to address a key aspect of management – the need to assess critically on a regular basis the effects of one's policies.

A *value-added service centre* treasury will aim to make a profit contribution by selectively hedging exposures within clearly defined parameters. While speculation will be forbidden, the typical value-added service centre treasury will be permitted to run unhedged positions if it is expected that the organization will be able to benefit from favourable exchange rate movements. Clearly, if the treasury has the freedom to manage exposure in this active way there is increased scope for making wrong hedging decisions; some currencies may be hedged when in retrospect it would have been better to leave them exposed, while others that should have been hedged may have been left uncovered. It is because the value-added service centre approach carries a greater risk both of making the wrong decision and of reaping rewards if, by luck or judgement, hedges are arranged at the right time that it is essential to measure the results of the treasury's hedging strategies. The quantitative performance measures that are applied should, of course, reflect the treasury's operating constraints (for example, the risk management parameters and permitted hedging instruments) as well as the resources available for exposure management and analysis.

The *profit centre* treasury aims to generate a profit contribution not simply through the management of the exposures that are generated by the company's trading activities but also through the deliberate creation of new exposures. Because, in the final analysis, the only justification for the actions of the profit centre treasury in *increasing* risk in this way is the profit that results, it is necessary to measure the benefits that flow from such risk-taking. Performance measurement is therefore an essential part of the control process in a profit centre treasury. If the rewards do not justify the risks that are taken, the company should change the role of the treasury to make it more risk averse. In a profit centre treasury, therefore, the emphasis of performance measurement should be primarily on quantifying the effects of its dealing activities; quality of service will be of secondary importance.

A further reason for measuring performance in a profit centre treasury is that the dealers' pay or bonuses may be dependent upon the profits that are produced. Performance measurement will then be necessary for the purpose of calculating profit-related pay.

The approach to performance measurement should, ideally, follow a structured course that will enable the activities measured and the benchmarks used to be both relevant to the kind of treasury that is being operated and applied at the appropriate level in the organization. There are four steps to achieving this. These are outlined below.

The approach to performance measurement

The company should decide how important it is to measure treasury performance and what it is (in general terms) that it wishes to measure. Thus it may want to measure the treasury's effectiveness in implementing policy, its efficiency in carrying out procedures or its economic contribution (the 'value added' by the treasury). One reason for measuring the treasury might, for example, be to assess whether the activities might be better performed on a centralized, or decentralized, basis or even outsourced to a third party.

Identification of the purpose of performance measurement

Measurement could take place at a number of levels. For example, in organizations where the hedging decision is under the control of subsidiaries, the financial outcome of the timing of transactions will be the responsibility of each subsidiary, and measurement should be performed at that level. If, however, the transactions are carried out by a central treasury at the request of subsidiaries, the efficiency with which deals are arranged, confirmed and settled will be the responsibility of the treasury

At what level should measurement take place?

and qualitative measures should be applied to measure the treasury's performance.

What activities should be measured?

The activities to be measured should be directly under the control of the individuals or departments being measured. As far as currency exposure is concerned, this is likely to cover, as a minimum, the management of transaction exposure (both committed and forecast) and translation exposure, as well as controls compliance.

What benchmarks are appropriate?

The benchmarks for measuring treasury performance are likely to depend upon the type of treasury being measured. The emphasis of performance measurement can be expected to be chiefly influenced by the appetite for risk of the organization. The relative importance, for example, of the quality of service to group companies will vary inversely to the degree of risk assumed by the treasury.

Criteria for setting benchmarks

Before the company identifies specific benchmarks, it should consider the criteria that the benchmarks should satisfy. These criteria are summarized below.

The benchmarks should encourage the right behaviour

Benchmarks must be consistent with the objectives and policies. A risk averse profit centre treasury should therefore use benchmarks that both reflect the constraints on its ability to manage risk actively and do not encourage the dealers to take positions or speculate. Where there are benchmarks for measuring the quality of service that the treasury provides to group companies, these should allow the treasury to implement the necessary controls properly and not provide an incentive to circumvent established procedures.

They should be achievable

Benchmarks must be achievable but demanding. If they are too easy to meet, they will be inadequate measures of performance as the treasury will not have to exert itself to achieve the targets. If, on the other hand, they are unrealistically difficult, the treasury may not attempt to achieve them and this will defeat their purpose.

They should be robust and durable

Benchmarks should be capable of being appropriate for a period of time so that valid comparisons can be made with performance in previous periods or from year to year.

Performance reporting will be provided to senior management who generally are not foreign exchange experts. Simple measures, rather than those based on complex technical data or sophisticated financial instruments, should be used so that they are readily understandable to their audience.

They should be simple and understandable

Simple benchmarks should also have the merit of being easy to calculate, because they are based on commonly available information and do not require sophisticated analytical techniques (which, if used, might increase the risk of error). The organization should therefore aim to use simple, easily calculated performance measures.

They should be easy to calculate

Two major benefits of performance measurement are that it can assist the identification of weaknesses or shortcomings and indicate what remedial action might be effective.

They should assist actions for improvement

Performance measurement might identify, for example, that:

- exposure forecasting is inaccurate
- exchange rate forecasts are unreliable
- hedging strategies are inappropriate
- service to group companies is inefficient, or
- control procedures are not implemented effectively.

The identification of these problems should prompt management action to improve forecasting techniques, refine its hedging strategies or provide additional resources as it deems appropriate to meet each problem.

Benchmarks must be achievable but demanding.

A practical approach to performance measurement, therefore, should have the following features. The benchmarks themselves should be recognized by the treasury staff as fair, achievable and appropriate for the operating environment. The measurement system should use simple data that are already available or which are obtainable with minimal effort and cost. Reporting should be standardized so that the same comparisons are made from one report to the next and information should be produced as quickly as possible so that, where necessary, remedial action can be taken with minimum delay. This requirement strengthens the case for simple measures; excessive complexity will slow the process, both in the production of information and in its interpretation. The aim should be to provide focused information on the key issues rather than extensive detail on relatively unimportant matters.

Performance measures

As has been mentioned earlier, a mixture of *quantitative* and *qualitative* performance measures should be used in assessing treasury performance. Quantitative measures will be relatively more important in those organizations with a greater appetite for risk while qualitative measures will be emphasized in risk averse companies.

Quantitative measures

Quantitative measures are used to assess the financial effects of the exposure management strategy that has been followed; such measures may be either *absolute* or *relative*. Absolute measures are fixed for a period of time, which may be anywhere between a month and a year while relative measures fluctuate with movements in the foreign exchange market. A commonly used absolute quantitative measure is the company's budget exchange rate, while a relative measure might be the average spot rate within a particular period.

Budget exchange rates

A company may decide that it will measure all hedging against the benchmark of the budget exchange rate that has been set at, or before, the beginning of the financial year for each currency in which it has exposures. This is an approach that is often taken, on the basis that budgeted profits from cross border operations depend upon the achievement of a particular exchange rate and that it is the treasury's job to deliver that rate.

Using a budget exchange rate as the benchmark can, however, lead to a number of difficulties. The rate may have been realistic when it was set, perhaps at an early stage in the development of the budget, but now not be achievable in the market. Alternatively, the budget rate may, indeed, reflect the current spot rate but forward cover can only be taken at significantly worse rates. In such circumstances the treasury, if it has discretion not to cover, will be tempted to leave exposures unhedged in the hope that exchange rates will move in a favourable direction. If this happens, the benchmark will cause a higher level of risk to be run than might otherwise have been the case. If it is obliged by the company's policies to hedge, the treasury will be forced to lock into exchange rates that are worse than its benchmark and will automatically have registered a 'poor' performance. If, on the other hand, rates have moved favourably and it is possible to hedge at budget rates or better the treasury may be tempted to cover all its exposures so as to lock into rates which will enable it to report good performance. This may turn out to be a mistake, as the opportunity will then have been lost to benefit from any further improvements in rates.

Another kind of absolute measure is the 'portfolio' rate. This assumes that the budgeted exposures could have been hedged at the outset of the year at currently available market rates. An average exchange rate for the year is then calculated for each currency based on the weighted currency flows and this rate is used as the benchmark. While this approach suffers from some of the disadvantages of the budget exchange rate in that it may encourage extremes of either fully hedging or leaving exposures uncovered, it does at least reflect the actual spot and forward rates available in the market at the time it is set and, because of this, meets the criterion of being achievable.

Portfolio rates

Each of these approaches, which effectively set the benchmark for a year ahead, assume both that the treasury has full discretion as to whether to hedge or not to hedge and that the budgeted or forecast currency exposures are a reliable basis for hedging. While it is possible to find treasuries (typically towards the profit centre end of the spectrum) that have such discretion, there are few that would feel confident enough in the accuracy of their forecasts to commit themselves to being fully hedged. In cases where a high degree of hedging does take place, a relatively significant proportion of it may be in the form of options to allow for inaccuracies in the forecast.

Where a company recognizes the shortcomings of using budget or portfolio rates it may turn to shorter term, but still absolute, rates as benchmarks. These might be monthly book-keeping rates based, for example, on the spot rate at the close of the previous month or they may be current market rates used to determine foreign currency prices for sales to overseas customers. In both cases the objective of the treasury will be to cover the resulting currency exposure at a rate as good as, or better than, the book-keeping or 'pricing' rate which serves as the benchmark. Because these benchmarks are based upon available market rates at the time they are set and cover a period for which exposures are likely to be committed (because they will predominantly relate to firm orders or sales) they meet the criteria for achievability and simplicity and enable the treasury to hedge with confidence; these benchmarks are therefore frequently found in use in the treasuries of companies that conduct their commercial activities on this basis.

Risk-adjusted absolute measures

A number of treasuries, typically those that are profit centres or strongly profit orientated, use what are described as risk-adjusted absolute measures. These measures calculate the Value at Risk of a particular transaction and set a hurdle return that must be met. This can be illustrated by the following example:

Example Risk-adjusted absolute performance measure

A profit centre treasury wishes to speculate on a strengthening of the US Dollar against Sterling over a six months' time horizon.

It intends to buy Dollars forward in the expectation of making a profit when it closes the contract out on maturity.

Assumptions:

- the $/£ exchange rate has 10 per cent annual standard deviation (approximately 7 per cent for six month volatility)

- the six month forward rate is $1.5300

- the company accepts a 97.5 per cent confidence level (two standard deviations).

At this risk tolerance the $/£ rate could move adversely to $1.7440 over the six month horizon. This would cost the company £12.3 million on a position of £100 million (£100 million at $1.5300 = $153 million; $153 million sold at $1.7440 = £87.7 million). The capital at risk is therefore £12.3 million.

If the treasury goes ahead and is able to close out the $153 million at, for example, a rate of $1.5200 it will receive £100 657 890. The profit of £657 890 represents an annualized return of 10.7 per cent on its risk capital of £12.3 million.

The performance benchmark should determine whether this is an acceptable return for the capital at risk.

Relative measures reflect changing market rates and are expressed in terms of the rate that would have been achievable had a particular course of action been taken by the treasury. The most commonly used relative measures are:

● **The forward rate at the time that a committed exposure was first identified**

The fact that the exposure is considered to be committed rather than merely forecasted is important, because at that point there is no reason (other than the desire to benefit from favourable movements in exchange rates) why it should not be covered immediately. The decision not to hedge is therefore interpreted as signifying the treasury's judgement that a better rate can be obtained by running the exposure.

If, for example, the treasury recognizes a committed US Dollar liability due in three months' time which can be hedged immediately against Sterling at a rate of $1.5300, this rate will be the benchmark against which the actual exchange rate that is eventually achieved will be measured. The treasury will

> *A number of treasuries use risk-adjusted absolute measures.*

therefore know, throughout the period that it is running the exposure, what the benchmark is and will be able to monitor opportunities to arrange forward cover at a rate better than the benchmark.

● **The spot rate at the time that a currency receipt or payment is settled**

This is the reverse of the example above (in which the benchmark aims to measure the effect of not hedging); in this case the benchmark measures the effect of hedging. The implicit assumption in measuring performance in this way is that taking action to hedge forward rather than waiting for the exposure to crystallize and then settling it at the prevailing spot rate suggests that the treasury expects to achieve a better rate by taking forward cover.

The main disadvantage of using the spot rate at maturity as the benchmark is that this rate will, of course, not be known until the last possible moment. The treasury will therefore be running the exposure without knowing what rate it will be judged against. The incentive, furthermore, will generally be for the treasury to deal at spot because it can then guarantee that it meets the target rate. The effect of this, however, will be to maximize the company's risk because a higher level of exposure will be run than if other benchmarks (which encouraged the treasury to hedge the exposure) were used.

- **The average spot rate for the period**

Many companies attempt to construct a more representative benchmark by using the average spot rate for the period in question. The thinking behind this is that this most closely reflects the range of hedging possibilities open to the treasury and therefore constitutes a more realistic benchmark. While the average spot rate has the merit of taking account of movements in market rates within the period under review, it nevertheless suffers from the disadvantages of not being known at the outset and, if the currency of exposure is at enough of a premium, perhaps not being achievable whichever hedging strategy was adopted.

One effect of using an average spot rate for the benchmark could be that the treasury hedges exposures in small amounts at intervals over the period in an attempt to achieve an average cover rate. This would, of course, result in greatly increased administrative costs and, probably, a worsening of the rates achieved as smaller sized deals tend not to attract the best prices.

Qualitative measures

Qualitative measures are used to assess the efficiency and effectiveness with which treasury activities are carried out. The treasury provides a service to group entities and carries out certain administrative procedures in support of the dealing process regardless of its position on the profit/cost centre spectrum; it is therefore appropriate to measure such activities using quantitative benchmarks in all types of treasury.

Qualitative measurement should assess a variety of aspects of the treasury's operations, including the accuracy of forecasting, deal execution and the provision of information to its group customers. Customer satisfaction is an important concept because it is a measure of efficiency; one way of measuring customer satisfaction objectively is to establish and evaluate performance against service levels that have been formally agreed between the treasury and its group customers.

The sort of activities that are most frequently the subject of qualitative performance measurement are outlined below.

The accuracy of exposure forecasting

The accuracy of exposure forecasting is vital to the effectiveness of risk management. If the forecast is wrong this will result either in exposures not being hedged or, alternatively, hedges being put in place needlessly, with the resulting costs of closing them out or rolling them over when they mature.

Forecasts should be constantly monitored for the accuracy of the timings, amounts and currencies of exposures. If the forecasts are generated by individual subsidiaries or divisions, inaccuracies should be traced by the treasury back to their source so that the reasons for errors can be identified and remedied. Measuring the accuracy of exposure forecasting is an activity that can enhance the whole risk management process if it leads to improvements in the quality of the information upon which policies, strategies and hedges are based.

> *Qualitative measures are used to assess the efficiency and effectiveness with which treasury activities are carried out.*

From the group customer's point of view it is important that the treasury should provide an efficient service when it requires an exposure to be hedged. The customer will therefore expect, and the treasury should be measured against:

The efficiency of deal execution

- the deal to be executed without delay after an authorized request for cover has been issued

- transactions to be arranged with competitive banks at best available rates

- cover to be transacted at the agreed rate if an order to deal or stop loss level has been requested

- immediate confirmation that the deal has been transacted with full details of the rate, bank and settlement instructions, and

- the efficient provision of accurate instructions to the banks without delay.

The above activities are those that are most commonly measured but this does not form an exhaustive list; other aspects of the relationship may also merit measurement if they are particularly important within an organization.

While some of the processes involved in deal administration have been captured in the list shown above, there are some activities that will not be visible to the treasury's group customers (perhaps, for example, because they relate to transactions that arise centrally, such as hedging interest on foreign currency debt or simply because they are not part of the service provided directly to those customers) but which nonetheless need to be performed efficiently. These activities might include:

The efficient completion of deal administration

- entering the transaction into the treasury system on the day of dealing

- confirming to the bank counterparty on the day of dealing (or within a specified time period)

- ensuring receipt and reconciliation of incoming counterparty confirmations (even though this is performed outside the treasury), and

- providing complete and accurate information for accounting and management reporting purposes in accordance with laid down timing requirements.

The efficiency with which all of these processes is carried out should also be assessed.

The provision of advice and information to the group

A key role of the treasury is as a source of advice to the group on all matters relating to currency management. Therefore, operating subsidiaries might expect to rely on the treasury for information about such matters as exchange controls, foreign banking and funds transmission arrangements, the outlook for the exchange rates of particular currencies, currency pricing implications and appropriate hedging instruments and techniques. They will assess the treasury both on its willingness to provide such help and the accuracy or reliability of the information provided. While it would be difficult to measure objectively the quality of the service provided in these respects, it is likely that group customers would nevertheless form an opinion on the value provided by the treasury and express such an opinion through the extent to which they continued to seek such advice.

> *A key role of the treasury is to advise the group on currency management.*

If the treasury is perceived to be failing in this area, this should be recognized and action taken to rectify the situation.

Provision of other management information

Management reporting for risk assessment and performance measurement purposes will provide much of the basic information that senior management requires simply to understand what transactions the treasury has entered into. There may, however, be other information that management requires for it to understand all aspects of the exposure management process.

This information is likely to relate mainly to the banking relationships that arise from hedging activity and which management will need to understand when negotiating facilities and discussing how to improve dealing performance both internally and with bank counterparties. The kind of information required for each includes:

- deals outstanding by currency pair, amount, exchange rate and value date

- the number of times the bank has been asked to quote, split by currency pair and spot, forward, currency option or other derivative contract, and

- the success rate for each bank split by currency pair and transaction type and shown on the basis both of the number of transactions and their value.

This information will show, for example, whether a bank is more competitive for spot deals or forward deals and whether it has won a small number of high value transactions or a large number of low value deals. This kind of analysis enables the treasury to select the most competitive banks to be quoted for any given type of transaction and therefore increases the likelihood of obtaining the best available rates in the market.

Monitoring compliance with controls

A key function of management reporting is to provide the information to senior management (ideally to the board or a delegated sub-committee, such as the Treasury Committee but often solely to the finance director) that enables it to fulfil its role of monitoring compliance with policies and controls. Information about the implementation of hedging policies will primarily be conveyed through the risk assessment and performance measurement reports described above. These reports will not normally address the subject of compliance with management controls and there will thus be a need to report separately on this aspect of the treasury's activities. Such reporting is often presented in the form of an exception report; only breaches of the controls are reported, but there should be explanation of why the breach occurred and what action has been taken as a result. The key activities that should be reported upon, if they are not already adequately covered elsewhere, are set out below. In all cases, of course, the target should be zero breaches.

Compliance with internal authority limits

Internal limits are designed to ensure that the company is not committed to transactions for significant amounts or in particular instruments without approval being given at an appropriately senior level. A breach of such a control is clearly a serious matter and should be notified to senior management without delay. In some companies the action taken against staff responsible for such a breach (without having a good excuse) can include instant dismissal.

Compliance with bank counterparty limits

The limits are intended to control the company's exposure to the risk of loss from bank failure. Any breach of limits should give the reason (which may be a 'technical' one arising, for example, from a movement in exchange rates that revalues an outstanding transaction in terms of the company's base currency) and the action taken, such as a temporary increase in the limit.

All transactions logged in company's records

Most companies set a time limit within which transactions must be recorded. This is normally on the dealing day or within one business day. It is important to record transactions speedily so that the company's exposures and risks at any particular moment are accurately identified. The use of sequentially numbered deal tickets assists the monitoring of transaction recording as it makes it easy to check that the full sequence of used deal tickets can be accounted for.

The report should confirm that the deal recording process has been completed comprehensively and within the prescribed time constraints.

Outward confirmation of all transactions

As discussed in Chapter 8, all deals should be confirmed in writing as soon as possible after they are struck and the confirmations should be produced and signed independently of the dealers. Compliance reporting should confirm that outward confirmation is being carried out in conformity with established control requirements.

Receipt of incoming counterparty confirmations

Reconciliation of incoming counterparty confirmations with the company's records is essential to the identification of unauthorized transactions and errors. Controls compliance reporting should therefore tell senior management that confirmations are received within the specified time periods, have all been received and that either no discrepancies have been detected or that any discrepancies have been satisfactorily resolved.

The report should identify any failures to complete settlement or delays in settlement, with explanations of the causes and remedial action taken, including where necessary interest claims in compensation.

Frequency of reporting

The frequency with which reports should be prepared will differ according to the information and the recipients. As a general rule, the treasury will need to generate reports that are essential to managing risk on a daily basis. Thus position reports giving details of exposures and counterparty limit utilization should be produced each day for the use of the treasury staff. This information should probably be provided to the finance director each week, but will not need to be provided to the board or Treasury Committee more frequently than monthly.

Similarly, controls compliance should be monitored on a daily basis by the treasurer and immediate action taken if a breach occurs. Breaches need not necessarily be reported to senior management as soon as they are identified, particularly if they are of a technical nature and established procedures are being followed to deal with the situation. Serious breaches of controls, which could result in significant financial loss, should, of course, always be reported to the most appropriate senior level as soon as they are identified.

It is good practice that all management reports, whoever they are provided to, should conform to a standardized format so that the recipients can become familiar with their content and easily compare one period with another. Reporting packages that change from issue to issue confuse the reader and make the tasks of assimilating and interpreting vital information and formulating appropriate action in response more time consuming and difficult. As noted earlier, a brief commentary to the numbers presented can draw out the key issues in each report and enhance its value considerably.

The treasury will need to generate reports that are essential to managing risk on a daily basis.

Difficulties with performance measurement

The extent to which performance measurement is carried out in corporate treasuries varies from country to country and according to the type of treasury being operated. Surveys have revealed that treasuries in countries such as France, Sweden and Norway tend to measure treasury performance more, and use more sophisticated measures to do so, than treasuries in, for example, Germany and the Netherlands. Performance measurement in the UK comes somewhere in between these two groups and is practised by approximately two-thirds of companies with dedicated treasury departments.

Those companies that do not measure performance give a number of reasons for their failure to do so. The most common reason is the difficulty in setting appropriate and relevant benchmarks. Other reasons given are the cost of the management time involved, the necessity of obtaining sophisticated (and expensive) systems to support the process and the perceived imbalance of cost against likely benefit that would result.

While it is certainly true that effective performance measurement does take time and resources, this may not be the whole story. Many treasurers would feel vulnerable having their performance held up to scrutiny by non-specialists using the benefit of hindsight. They might well ask why their colleagues in other disciplines are not measured in the same way. They might also be able to claim, at the risk of being found to blame, that there are no established treasury objectives, policies and controls against which they could be measured. If that really were the case, the question of performance measurement would have identified the most fundamental of all treasury issues and have pointed the way to the action necessary to set the company's foreign exchange exposure management on a firm foundation for the future.

At this point we have completed the foreign exchange exposure management cycle. It started at risk identification, proceeded through the formulation and implementation of objectives, policies and procedures within a system of controls, and ends with the monitoring, analysis and reporting that confirm that the treasury has followed the path set for it by the board.

Management reporting is a key part of the currency exposure management process. It should provide the information that enables the board and senior management to satisfy themselves that the approved exposure management process is being followed and to assess its results. Where the analysis of dealing performance suggests that a change in approach is required, the reporting processes should enable the appropriate remedial action to be identified.

Summary

Management reporting should satisfy all the following four requirements:

- the assessment and management of risk
- the identification of the financial effects of the hedging strategy and the measurement of treasury efficiency
- the need for information about hedges and outstanding positions, and
- to confirm compliance with control procedures.

Performance measurement should take into consideration the role of the treasury and the resources devoted to it. Benchmarks should encourage the right behaviour and be achievable, durable, simple, and easy to calculate. They should also assist action for initiating improvements where shortcomings have been identified. Performance measures can be both quantitative and qualitative – a treasury should aim to have the right mix of measures to meet its particular requirements.

It is particularly important to report on compliance with controls. If no one is checking that controls are being implemented no one will know when they are being ignored.

Glossary of terms

Actual exposure A currency receipt or payment that will definitely take place because it results from a firm order or sale for which an invoice or other documentation has been issued.

American option A currency option that can be exercised at any time up to its expiry date.

Appreciation An increase in the value of a currency in relation to other currencies.

Arbitrage (1) Dealing in two centres to make a gain by exploiting a temporary difference in rates between two places. (2) Creating cheaper funds in a currency by borrowing another currency and converting them by means of a swap transaction into the currency required while at the same time hedging forward the reconversion into the original currency.

Arbitrageur A person who engages in arbitrage.

At-best An order to a bank to buy or sell foreign exchange at the most favourable rate.

At-the-money An option in which the exercise (or 'strike') price is equal to the market price of the underlying asset. A currency option is described as 'at-the-money forward' when the exercise price is equal to the forward rate for its maturity date and 'at-the-money spot' when the current spot rate is equal to the exercise price. European options, which can only be exercised on their expiry date, are often sold 'at-the-money forward' and American options, which can be exercised at any time, are sold 'at-the-money spot'.

Average rate option An AVRO allows the purchaser to be protected against adverse movements in the exchange rate relative to the strike rate while at the same time allowing him to benefit from favourable movements in rates. A strike rate is agreed for the AVRO and this is compared with the average rate over the period, calculated by reference to an accepted marker rate such as the central bank fixing rate for the currency pair.

Band The range of fluctuation permitted for a currency against another currency under an international agreement.

Barrier option *See* 'knock-out option'.

Base currency (1) A single unit of one currency which is used as the base against which another currency's value is expressed. For example, in the quotation £1 = DEM2.3570, Sterling is the base currency. Also known as the 'quote currency'. (2) The domestic, accounting or functional currency of an entity, against which all other currencies represent foreign exchange exposures.

Bid The rate at which a potential purchaser offers to buy a currency.

Big figure   Rates are usually quoted to four decimal places; e.g. £1 = $1.5436. The last two digits, 36, are known as 'points' (or 'pips'), the next, 4, is the 'big figure', and the first three digits, 1.54, are the 'big figures'.

Bloc   *See* 'currency bloc'.

Blocked currency   A currency that is subject to exchange controls or transfer restrictions by the government of issue.

Bretton Woods   Agreement made at Bretton Woods, New Hampshire, USA, in July 1944 to provide a stable monetary environment to aid economic reconstruction after the Second World War. The agreement, signed by 44 countries, established the International Monetary Fund and set up a fixed rate system of foreign exchange rates for most of the major currencies of the world.

Broken date   Also known as an 'odd date' or 'cock date'. A broken date is a maturity date that falls between straight dealing dates; for example, two months and four days, which is between the two and three month straight dates. Broken date quotes are based on interpolation between straight date prices.

Broker   An intermediary acting between banks or a bank and a corporate customer in order to bring together two parties to a transaction. Brokers do not take their own positions and earn their return from brokerage fees.

Business day   Any day on which business can be conducted in a particular foreign exchange market. Also known as a 'clear day'.

Buyer   The purchaser of an option or of currency.

Buying rate   The rate at which a bank is prepared to buy a foreign currency. Also known as the 'bid' rate.

Cable   Shorthand expression used in the foreign exchange market for the US Dollar/Sterling spot rate. The term originates from the early days of the market when a cable was sent each day from New York to London to advise the rate at which the Dollar was trading against Sterling in New York.

Call option   Used in respect of options where the buyer has the right to buy the underlying currency or instrument at an agreed price during a specified period from the other party to the transaction.

Changes or 'changing'   Term used by dealers to advise customers that they are no longer prepared to deal at a previously quoted rate. This might occur if a deal is being quoted competitively in a moving market and a bank needs to change its quoted rate because the market has moved.

Chooser options   Also known as 'double options', these are not specified at origination as calls or puts. The purchaser can choose, at a specified date, whether the option is to be a put or call.

Closing trade   A deal that matches or closes an existing open position.

Committed exposure   Same as 'actual exposure'.

Compensation   The settlement of a maturing forward foreign exchange contract by offsetting an opposite contract for an equal amount of currency. Compensation contracts are used either when the currency is not available to settle the original contract, in which case the contract is closed out, or to extend cover to another date, in which case using a swap transaction the contract is 'compensated and extended' ('comp and extend'). Also known as a 'rollover' transaction.

Compound option   An option on an option. A buyer of a compound option pays a premium for the first leg of the structure, which is known as the compound call. This gives the buyer the right, but not the obligation, to buy a specified ordinary option at a pre-determined price on a pre-determined future date (the second leg). A buyer will normally only exercise the right to buy the second leg if the same option cannot be bought more cheaply elsewhere at the time.

Confirmation letter   A written record of a transaction sent by each counterparty to the other. The confirmation sets out each party's understanding of the transaction and should be reconciled to ensure that there is no disagreement about the transaction undertaken. Written confirmations are increasingly being replaced by electronic deal matching systems.

Contract date   The date on which a contract is agreed to. (Same as deal date and transaction date.)

Convertible currency   A currency that may be exchanged for another currency without being subject to official restrictions.

Convertibility   The quality ascribed to a currency in being convertible.

Copey   Dealers' slang expression for the Danish Krone, from 'Copenhagen'.

Correspondent bank   A bank or other financial institution that provides banking services to another bank in a territory where the second bank does not have its own representation.

Counterparty   Each principal in a foreign exchange transaction. For example, when a corporate customer buys currency from a bank, the bank is its counterparty.

Countervalue   The amount that results from the sale or purchase of a specified amount of currency. For example, if US Dollars 1 000 000 were bought against Sterling at a rate of $1.52 the countervalue would be £657 894.73.

Cover   The purchase or sale of foreign currency to meet spot or future commitments or to close out an open or short position in a currency.

Covered interest arbitrage   The simultaneous spot sale or purchase of foreign currency with the forward purchase or sale of the currency in which a borrowing or investment has been made. This transaction (a swap transaction) removes the foreign exchange risk for a borrowing or investment in foreign currency.

Cross rate   The exchange rate between two currencies neither of which is the dealing entity's base currency. For example, a British bank in London quoting a French Franc/Deutsche Mark cross rate.

Currency basket   A collection of currencies that are individually weighted and combined to create a unit of another currency; for example, the European Currency Unit, the ECU, being a basket of a number of European currencies.

Currency bloc   A group of currencies that are, officially or unofficially, linked and as a result move together in the foreign exchange market.

Currency option   A contract which, for the payment of a fee, confers upon the buyer the right, but not the obligation, to deliver or take delivery of a specified amount of currency at a specified rate at or up to a specified maturity date. *See also* 'option contract'.

Cylinder option   A currency option that involves the simultaneous purchase and sale of options to buy and sell the same amount of currency at different strike rates. The objective in entering into a cylinder option is to reduce or eliminate the option premium. Also known as a 'zero cost' or 'range forward'.

Daylight exposure   The net mismatch of the sales and purchases of each currency traded by a bank in its foreign exchange dealing during a working day.

Deal   A single foreign exchange transaction.

Deal date   The date on which a deal was transacted.

Deal ticket   Written record of a transaction completed by the dealer at the time of dealing and passed by the dealer to the back office for processing. Deal tickets are usually sequentially numbered. The deal ticket forms the primary record of each transaction and is a vital part of the audit trail.

Dealer   A person employed by a company or bank engaged in dealing in foreign exchange as a principal who is authorized to arrange transactions on behalf of his employer.

Delivery date   The date on which funds must be delivered to settle a transaction. Same as maturity, settlement and value date.

Delta   The expected change in the option premium for a one unit change in the price of the underlying asset. The delta of an option is the main determinant of the risk factors used by exchanges in calculating the margin funds that must be deposited by option sellers and buyers.

Depth of market   The extent to which transactions may easily be arranged in the market without affecting the rate. *See* 'stable market' and 'thin market'.

Derivative   A financial instrument the value of which depends on, or is derived from, the price movements in one or more underlying assets (such as currencies). Derivatives can be traded on an exchange or 'over the counter' (OTC). Exchange traded contracts are typically for standard amounts and delivery dates whereas an OTC contract is more flexible and tailored to the user's requirements.

Digital options   Also known as 'binary options', these have only two possible outcomes: a zero pay-off if they expire out-of-the-money and a pre-determined value if they expire in-the-money.

Discount   A currency is at a discount to another currency if its forward rate is weaker than the spot rate. This results from it having a higher interest rate than the other currency. The discount on the forward exchange rate offsets the higher interest rate so that no net benefit can be gained by swapping from one currency into another on a fully covered basis.

Economic exposure   Economic exposure (also known as strategic exposure) comprises a range of factors, including the geographical locations in which a company operates, the locations of its competitors, the hedging strategies of its competitors and differences in exchange rate movements between competing currencies. Economic exposure may be direct, when a foreign supplier is competing against a local supplier in a particular market, or indirect, for example when foreign suppliers from two different countries are competing against each other in a third country. The relative strength of the competing suppliers' currencies will give each supplier an economic exposure – in some cases this will be advantageous, in other cases it will be a disadvantage.

ECU   European Currency Unit. An artificial currency created by reference to a weighted basket of European currencies. The ECU is used for accounting and funding purposes within the EU and can also be used as a hedging currency where a single contract is required to hedge exposures in a variety of the ECU's constituent currencies.

Effective exchange rate   A composite rate that reflects a currency's performance on a trade weighted basis against its main competitors. The effective exchange rate is normally expressed as an index.

Either way price   A quote with no spread, the buying rate being the same as the selling rate.

EMS   European Monetary System.

ERM   Exchange Rate Mechanism of the EMS, the arrangement by which member currencies are tied to each other within defined bands of fluctuation.

Eurocurrency   A freely convertible currency that is held outside its currency of issue and is thus not subject to exchange controls. For example, Eurodollars held in London by a branch of an American bank.

Eurodollar   A US Dollar denominated account held in a bank (including a branch of a US bank) located outside of the USA. *See* Eurocurrency.

Exchange controls   Restrictions on the convertibility of a currency, imposed either by government or a central bank.

Exchange control risk   The risk that a contract for future delivery of currency may be blocked by the imposition of exchange controls.

Exchange rate   The rate at which one currency is exchanged for another.

Exchange risk   *See* transaction exposure.

Exchange traded option   An option traded on a recognised exchange. Exchange traded, or 'listed', options are available only in multiples of a pre-determined standard amount and are limited to specified currencies and maturity dates. Most exchange traded options are American options.

Exercise price   The strike price (or strike rate) of an option.

Exotic currency   A currency that does not have a developed international market and is infrequently dealt.

Expiration month   The dates on which options, particularly exchange traded options, expire.

Expiry date   The final date in the life of an option on which it can be exercised.

Exposure management   The process of minimizing the financial effects of changes in exchange rates using internal and external hedging techniques.

Fair value   The option value derived from a mathematical option valuation model.

Firm   (1) A market in which prices are strengthening or rising. (2) A quote at which a dealer is prepared to trade.

Fixed dates   *See* 'straight dates'.

Fixed exchange rate system   A system under which a government (or other official body) intervenes in the exchange market to maintain its currency at a par value set by the government.

Fixing   In some foreign exchange markets, a daily meeting at which rates for different currencies are officially fixed in line with market prices. Participants in the daily fixing typically include the central bank and the main commercial banks.

Floating   The absence of fixed intervention rates and little or no official control over the market. In a freely floating market, exchange rates are determined predominantly by supply and demand.

Forecast exposure   Or uncommitted exposure. A currency exposure which is expected to arise, based on reasonable forecasts of future trading patterns.

Foreign exchange contract   A formal and binding agreement to purchase or sell a specified amount of a named currency against a specified amount of another currency at a firm rate for delivery and payment on or by a fixed date.

Forex or FX   Foreign exchange.

Forward book   The net position arising from all forward transactions in a particular currency.

Forward position   The net of forward purchases and inflows of currency and forward sales and outflows in the same currencies.

Forward contract   A contract to exchange a specified amount of one currency for a specified amount of another currency on an agreed future date. (*See* 'forward rate'.)

Forward option contract   A forward contract that matures within an agreed time period rather than on a particular value date. Also known as an 'option dated forward contract' or 'option contract'.

Forward rate   A rate at which a contract may be made to exchange one currency for another at a specified future date. The difference between the forward rate and the spot rate is termed the forward premium or discount.

Futures   Contracts entered into on an exchange to buy or sell a standard quantity of a specific asset at a pre-determined future date and at an agreed price. In practice, most futures' contracts are closed out at or before maturity and no physical delivery is performed.

Hard currency   A strong currency that is not subject to exchange controls and is easily convertible into other currencies.

Hedging (external)   The action of using foreign exchange contracts, currency options, derivative instruments or borrowings to fix in advance the exchange rate relating to future currency receipts, payments or balance sheet items thereby eliminating exposure to exchange rate movements.

Hedging (internal)   The action of arranging one's currency flows and positions so as to minimize net exposure to currency movements. An example of this is the offsetting of receipts in a currency by payments in the same currency.

Implied volatility   The value of asset price volatility that will equate the market price of an option to the fair value of an option.

Indicative rate   *See* 'level'. Also known as an 'indication rate' or 'info quote'.

Indirect quote   An exchange rate quotation in which the local currency is the base currency and the other currency is valued in terms of the local currency. For example, in France an indirect quotation is FRF1 = £0.12.

Instructions   The provision of details as to the banks to which funds shall be paid and received in settlement of a foreign exchange transaction.

Instrument   A foreign exchange market transaction that enables a currency to be converted, either directly or at the purchaser's option, into another currency either at spot or at a future date.

Interbank deal   A deal in which both counterparties are banks. Also known as a 'market deal'.

Interest rate differential   The difference between the interest rates in two currencies for an investment or borrowing with the same maturity.

Intervention   The buying and selling of currency in the foreign exchange markets by a government or central bank to support or change a currency's rate of exchange in pursuit of an economic or political policy.

In-the-money   An option is in-the-money if it has intrinsic value (i.e. the strike rate is better than the market rate spot or forward according to the type of option). A call is in-the-money if the asset price is above the exercise price and a put is in-the-money if the asset price is below the exercise price.

Intrinsic value   The amount of profit that would be realized if an option were to be exercised immediately.

Knock-out option   A knock-out option incorporates an exchange rate at which, if it is reached in the market, the option will become inoperative or 'knocked-out'. This rate is known as the knock-out level and the cost of the option is largely determined by how close the knock-out level is to the current spot rate. If the knock-out level is close to the spot rate, the option will be relatively cheap. The farther away from the spot rate it is the more expensive the option will be, and the closer its price will be to an ordinary option. A knock-out should, however, always be cheaper than an ordinary option.

Knock-out options are also known as 'barrier options'. Another kind of barrier option is the knock-in option, which becomes operative when a predetermined rate is reached in the market and which works in a similar way to the knock-out option.

Leading and lagging   The process of adjusting the timing of currency receipts and payments in order to create offsetting flows to reduce exposure.

Level   A non-binding quotation for information purposes that indicates the rate at which a currency is trading. Also known as an indicative, indication or info rate.

Long forward exchange   Forward transactions maturing in excess of three months.

Long position   An excess of purchases over sales, or of assets over liabilities in a currency.

Lookback option   A lookback option is similar to an average rate option but, instead of using average rates, uses the most favourable rate among all of the spot rates during its life. This feature of lookback options maximizes their volatility and makes them more expensive than comparable ordinary options.

Mandate   A formal written authority provided to a bank by a customer setting out the basis on which the bank is authorized to enter into foreign exchange transactions with the customer and effect settlement of them.

Margin   (1) The sum of money that must be deposited with a clearing house or broker by the writer of an option to protect the clearing house against his non-performance. (2) The difference between a dealer's buying and selling rates – the 'bid/ask' or 'bid/offer' margin. *See also* 'spread'.

Market amount   The minimum amount normally dealt in a currency between banks either direct or via brokers.

Mark to market   The revaluation of foreign exchange contracts and options at their current market value in order to reflect gains and losses resulting from market price movements.

Matching   The process of offsetting receipts and payments in the same currency with respect to amount and timing in order to minimize exposure.

Middle rate (or price)   The mid point between the buying and selling rate for a currency. Also known as the 'mid-rate'.

Milliard   One thousand million. For example, LIT 1 000 000 000. *See* 'yard'.

Mio   One million.

Netting   The process of offsetting currency receipts and payments across all currencies in order to derive the net long or short position in each currency.

Nostro account   A bank's current account with another bank.

Notice of exercise   Notice from the holder of an option of the intention to exercise the option.

Numeraire   A unit of value, such as the ECU or the SDR, which is not itself legal tender but is composed of units that are legal tender.

Odd date   *See* 'broken date'.

Odd lot   Interbank dealing is usually for round amounts. For example, $1 million. An odd amount of currency, that is not a round amount, is described as an 'odd lot'. The price on an odd lot deal will often be slightly worse than for a round amount.

Offer or 'Offered rate'   The rate at which a dealer is prepared to sell. Same as 'selling rate'.

Open position   An uncovered foreign exchange risk representing the difference between the long and short positions in a particular currency.

Opening transaction The purchase or writing of an option that establishes a new position.

Option contract (1) A contract that confers the right but not the obligation to buy or sell a specified quantity of a specified asset or currency at a fixed price at or before an agreed future date. (2) Same as a 'forward option contract'.

Out-of-the-money An option that has no intrinsic value. For a call option the exercise price is higher than the asset price; for a put the exercise price is lower than the asset price.

Outright (forward) deal The exchange of one currency for another at a future date rather than at the spot date; in other words, a forward contract.

Outright rate The rate for a forward contract, as distinct from its component parts, the spot rate and forward points.

Over the counter (OTC) A market that is external to a formal exchange in which transactions are arranged directly between principals and customers.

Par, or at Par Where the forward price is the same as the spot price. That is, there is no forward premium or discount.

Paris Dealers' slang expression for the French Franc.

Pay-later options Similar to an ordinary option, but no upfront fee is payable. If the option expires out-of-the-money, no premium is payable. If it expires in-the-money, a predetermined premium is payable. In this case the premium will be greater than that for an ordinary option.

Point In a foreign exchange rate it is one hundredth of one cent; i.e. in a rate quoted to four places a point is the fourth figure after the decimal point. For example, if the rate of 1.5346 changes to a rate of 1.5349 it is said to have moved 3 points.

'Forward points' are the number of points by which the spot rate must be adjusted to calculate the forward rate for a particular maturity date.

Premium (1) The price paid for the purchase of a currency option. (2) A currency is described as being at a premium to another currency if its forward rate against the currency is stronger than the spot rate.

Proxy currency A currency that is closely linked to another currency and may be hedged in place of the linked currency. For example, the Dutch Guilder and the Deutsche Mark are closely linked and the Deutsche Mark is often hedged as a proxy for the Guilder.

Put option The right of a purchaser of an option to sell the underlying currency or instrument, at an agreed rate during a specified period to the other party to the transaction.

Quotation (or quote) The bid or offered price of a currency or option in the market or on an exchange. A quote may be either firm (at which a dealer is prepared to trade) or indicative (provided for reference purposes).

Rating An evaluation of the creditworthiness of either a specific security or a borrower, made by a credit rating agency such as Moody's or Standard & Poor's. Corporate treasurers use credit ratings to control their exposure to counterparty risk.

Risk aversion The extent to which an organization will tolerate being exposed to exchange risk.

Rollover The extension of the life of a forward contract by compensating and extending it (*see* 'compensation' and 'swap contract'). When a contract is compensated it is likely that a small balance will be payable or receivable on the close out of the original contract as the exchange rate for the compensation contract will differ from that for the original deal.

Running a position Holding a long or short position in a currency in the hope of an exchange gain.

Same-day settlement A term used in the UK domestic market for cash settlement on the day of dealing.

SDR Special Drawing Right. A synthetic currency created by the International Monetary Fund and based on a weighted basket of the world's major currencies.

Seller The writer of an option, who thereby sells to a counterparty the right to buy or sell an asset to the seller of the option.

Selling rate *See* 'offer'.

Settlement The receipt of currency bought and the payment of currency sold in satisfaction of a foreign exchange contract on its maturity date.

Settlement date The date on which a transaction is settled. This date is the same as the 'delivery', 'maturity', and 'value date'.

Settlement risk The risk that a counterparty will fail to meet its obligations at the settlement of a foreign exchange contract.

SCOUT A shared currency option, under tender. This type of option enables tenderers to share the premium cost of an option while at the same time giving each tenderer full cover in the event that its tender is successful. This is effected by the awarder of the contract purchasing an option and charging the tenderers for an equal share of the premium cost. When the contract is awarded the successful tenderer takes over the option and is thus provided with full cover of the exposure.

Short dates The maturity dates for periods up to seven working days from the dealing date. These include overnight (today until tomorrow), tom/next (tomorrow to the day after), spot/next (the spot value date until the day after) and spot-a-week (spot value date to a calendar week after).

Short forward exchange Forward transactions maturing within one month.

Short position An excess of sales over purchases or liabilities over assets in a currency.

Soft currency A term used to describe a currency that is considered likely to depreciate in value. Also known as a 'weak' currency.

Spot-a-week *See* 'short dates'.

Spot contract A foreign exchange contract that matures either one day or two days (depending upon the currency involved) after the dealing date. For example, a Sterling/DEM spot contract matures two business days after dealing whereas a US Dollar/Canadian Dollar spot contract matures on the next business day after dealing.

Spot date   The date on which a spot contract matures and is settled.

Spot/next   *See* 'short dates'.

Spot rate   The rate for the purchase or sale of a currency for spot delivery.

Speculation   A deal made independently of any underlying commercial need with the objective of making profit. Speculation necessarily involves incurring additional risk, even if that risk is limited to the loss of a premium paid for the use of options and other derivatives. Speculation is the opposite of hedging.

Spread   The difference between buying and selling prices at which a transaction may take place. The spread is one source of a dealer's profit. *See also* 'margin'.

Stable market   An active market with a high turnover that can accommodate high value transactions without incurring appreciable movements in exchange rates. *See* 'depth of market' and 'thin market'.

Stocky   Dealers' slang expression for the Swedish Krona, from 'Stockholm'.

Straight dates   The whole month forward dates for which the market is quoting rates on any business day (also known as 'fixed dates').

Straddle   A combination of a put and a call option on the same underlying asset, each of which has the same exercise price and expiry date.

Strike price   Or strike rate. The same as 'exercise price', the rate at which an option buyer has the right to call or put a currency.

Strong currency   A currency that is considered likely to appreciate or maintain its value.

Swap contract   A pair of foreign exchange transactions in which there is a simultaneous purchase and sale of one currency against another for two different value dates. A swap may comprise a spot and a forward contract or two forward contracts. If the amounts of currency differ in the two halves of the contract, it is termed a mismatched swap. A swap contract is cheaper than two separate contracts because it is structured in a way that eliminates the bank's bid/ask spread.

Swap contracts are usually transacted to compensate and extend an existing contract or as part of a funding arbitrage action to obtain a cheaper source of funding in another currency and at the same time eliminate exchange risk.

This kind of swap contract should not be confused with an interest rate swap or with a currency swap on a borrowing in which the principal amount of the borrowing is swapped from one currency to another.

SWIFT   Society for Worldwide Interbank Financial Telecommunication. This is a non-profit-making organization owned by banks to enable reliable and independent worldwide communications principally for the transfer of funds.

Swissy   Dealers' slang expression for the Swiss Franc.

Tender to contract options   Tender to contract (TTC) options are designed for companies that are involved in tendering for very large contracts which would involve the payment of significant premiums if they were fully covered by options. The TTC option allows the buyer to pay only 10 per cent of the premium at the time of submitting the tender. The balance of the premium is payable only if the tender is successful. If the tender is unsuccessful, the option lapses and cannot be used against other tenders or exercised in the market.

Theta   The rate of change in an option price with the passage of time. It indicates the loss of value in the option as the expiry date approaches. Time decay is not constant over the life of an option; it tends to increase as the expiry date gets nearer.

Thin market   A market in which there is a low turnover or in which trading is nervous, where a significant transaction will result in a clear movement in the rate. Spreads are typically wide in a thin market as dealers are concerned about how easily they will be able to lay off any deal that has been done.

Time value   The amount by which an option's premium exceeds its intrinsic value.

Tom/next   *See* 'short dates'.

Transaction date   Or 'deal date'. The date on which a transaction is entered into or, in other words, the day on which the deal is 'struck'.

Transaction exposure   The risk that the base-currency value of a foreign-currency-denominated trading transaction will vary as a result of changes in exchange rates giving rise to an increase or decrease in reported profit.

Translation exposure   The risk that, when translated at the foreign exchange rates which will apply at a future balance sheet date, the domestic (or base) currency values of assets and liabilities on the balance sheet will alter, resulting in a reported gain or loss.

Value date   The date when the delivery of funds to settle a transaction is due (normally the maturity date of the transaction).

Value today   A foreign exchange transaction in which delivery and payment are made on the same day as the contract, instead of the normal spot value date one or two business days later. The spot rate is adjusted for a same-day value contract to reflect the earlier settlement.

Value tomorrow   A foreign exchange transaction in which delivery and payment are due on the next clear business day after the dealing date. Canadian Dollar/US Dollar spot transactions are normally made for value tomorrow.

Vega   A measure of the sensitivity of the option price to changes in the volatility of the underlying asset price. Increased volatility will result in a broadly linear increase in the volatility element of premium cost.

Volatility   The susceptibility of a rate to rapid movements.

Vostro account   A foreign bank's account with a local bank. For example, a German bank's account with a London bank will be a vostro account from the London bank's point of view. (To the German bank it is a nostro account.)

Writer   The seller of a call or put option in respect of an opening transaction.

Yard   Slang for milliard. For example, a yard of Lira is LIT 1 000 000 000.

Index

Index

Index